JOURNEYS TO SUCCESS
WOMEN'S EDITION
VOLUME 3

12 REAL-LIFE WOMEN SHARE
THEIR INSPIRING STORIES

Copyright © 2016 by John Westley Publishing

Publishers: John Westley Clayton

www.johnwestley.com

info@johnwestley.com

& Tom Cunningham

www.tom2tall.com

tom@tom2tall.com

ISBN 978-0-9976801-2-6

All Rights Reserved.

No part of this publication may be reproduced, distributed, or transmitted in any form or by any means, including photocopying, recording, or other electronic or mechanical methods, or by any information storage and retrieval system without the prior written permission of the publisher and/or individual contributing author, except in the case of very brief quotations embodied in critical reviews and certain other noncommercial uses permitted by copyright law.

CONTENTS

CONTENTS	i
DEDICATION	iii
TESTIMONIALS	iv
FOREWORD	vii
INTRODUCTION	xiv
MY MARRIAGE WITH FOOD AND FITNESS	1
By: Therese Cote	
NOT EVERYONE CHARGED WITH A CRIME IS GUILTY	10
By: Kim Cunningham	
MONEY TIPS FROM THE BAKER'S DAUGHTER	19
By: Chella Diaz	
ANOTHER LEAP OF FAITH	30
By: Kat Downey	
TO DREAM THE IMPOSSIBLE DREAM	40
By: Kathy Hadley	
MY JOURNEY TO THINK AND GROW RICH	55
By: Karren E. Henderson	
FROM ZERO TO HERO	63
By: Jessica Higdon	
BREAKING THE CYCLE	73
By: Sandra C. Pascal	
BEFORE THE RISE, COMES THE FALL	83
By: Hillary Vargas	

ACCEPT WHAT IS, LET GO OF WHAT WAS, AND HAVE FAITH IN YOUR JOURNEY   **91**
    By: Gisella Marie Vasquez

FALL DOWN SEVEN TIMES, STAND UP EIGHT   **101**
    By: Adrienne Mae Yu

NAPOLEON HILL BIO   **111**

DEDICATION

Although these stories are powerful testimonials written by women's perspective, men can also gain a better level of understanding and appreciation of the stress, strain, struggles and setbacks that come alongside with success. Which principle will you implement to impact your life?

-April Joy Ford

TESTIMONIALS

"So many of us have love to give, stories to tell, advice to share, and burdens to let go of. Nothing is more ancient or real than a tribe of women gathered in a circle, holding each other up and lifting each other high. Such is the primal sisterhood, one of the most powerful vortexes out of which emerges new life within and among us."

- Marianne Williamson

Marianne Williamson

Marianne Williamson is an internationally acclaimed author and lecturer. Six of her ten published books have been New York Times bestsellers. Her books include A Return to Love, A Year of Miracles, The Law of Divine Compensation, The Age of Miracles, A Course in Weight Loss, Everyday Grace, A Woman's Worth, Illuminata, and The Gift of Change. Marianne has been a popular guest on television programs such as Oprah, Good Morning America and Charlie Rose.

"Journey To Success – Women's Edition" is empowering and uplifting on every level. It is a must read for women everywhere who need to know that their efforts are not wasted. To quote Napoleon Hill, "Patience, persistence and perspiration make an unbeatable combination for success".

-Michelle Patterson

Michelle Patterson,
CEO Women Network LLC and the California Women's Conference.

Michelle Patterson is the CEO of Women Network LLC, a media and production company giving women a voice to share their message. Women Network is creating the largest community of women globally, and they are the exclusive event producer of the California Women's Conference.

Mrs. Patterson is also the founder of Women Network Foundation, a 501 (c)(3) non-profit public charity created to bring women together to create global change by empowering them to transform their communities. Its mission supports women to effectuate this change through serving as a worldwide conduit for connecting community, mentoring, education, and financial support.

FOREWORD
By: April Joy Ford

Wonder Woman's Faith Is Greater Than Her Fear

More women need to hear the success stories of other women. Often times we feel alone in our struggles and setbacks and wonder how other women have done it. What is her secret to success; managing work, home, and personal life?

Even with this book project, some women were hesitant to share their story or just even parts of their story. Why you might wonder…their reasons included; 'I don't want to offend another person involved in my story', 'nobody would want to hear my ordinary story', 'I've been writing my story for years now but waiting for the perfect time' or 'I have too much going on, I don't have time….' and more reasons we can list which are respectfully understandable.

But for those women who had the courage to share their stories even the intimate personal details in here and committed to collaborating, their stories after were more powerful. It was as if the actual writing process gave them their own power back and provided healing, insight and a greater perspective on how far they have actually come. If you are looking not only for the inspiration of authentic and real stories from struggle to success but also implementation, these stories are for you.

Sometimes women can be so hard on themselves for having the "Wonder Woman Syndrome". If you answer yes to at least 3 of these items then you probably have the Wonder Woman Syndrome:

Do you say yes to everything? Do you have a hard time saying no?

Do you have a hard time asking for help?

Do you overcompensate in different areas of your life; work, relationships, fitness, etc…?

Do you compromise in various areas of your life and it reflects in your health, dreams-goals, dating-relationships, etc?

Do you tend to be competitive with others or even yourself to be perfect?

This is called the Wonder Woman Syndrome because, from the outside, some women can appear to be the perfect superhero. This person obviously has everything together from her career, finances, family, and relationships as so it seems. However, deep inside this woman is feeling stress, anxiety, overwhelm, burned-out and maybe even depression.

So where would this syndrome root from?
The underlining common denominator equates to;

- Lacking boundaries
- Each woman just wants to feel accepted, loved and understood
- To feel connected
- To prove their worthiness or confidence
- Seeking approval and validation

Although having this syndrome might cause you to often feel depleted, drained and in a disaster, there is a bright side. It has given you the capacity to be more compassionate, loving, caring, forgiving and having the ultimate super power, faith.

The real Wonder Woman would know how to establish boundaries to say yes to what fits in alignment of her parameters and say no to anything else. Her boundaries create a healthy "balance" within the areas of her life without compromising her truth and values. The real wonder woman has the confidence to ask for help instead of feeling like she has the whole world on her shoulders, alone. The real wonder woman has the spirit of collaboration, not competition and shines her light to magnify the light of other women.

This collaborative publication is the fruit of what real wonder women go through to manage all their roles and responsibilities as women; from their struggles, setback, and challenges to achievements and success. Each author shares her personal journey and how she's implemented the success principles of Napoleon Hill. It was her bodacious faith that she committed to herself first that allowed her to persevere through all the negative self-talk, the nay-sayers, fear, doubt, worry, and stress.

Whether you have read Napoleon Hill's work before or not, you will find your favorite chapter in here and when that story speaks to you, identify which principle it is that you can implement in your own life.

The only way to grow is by stretching beyond our own limits. Imagine someone extending their arm towards yours to help pull you up and with your other arm, you're reaching out to pull another woman up. That is why these women in this book have shared their most personal stories from struggles to success to reach back and pay it forward for you.

It is interesting to see the diverse stories from various backgrounds, and each woman has their personal favorite success principle(s) from Napoleon Hill.

- Definiteness of Purpose
- Mastermind Alliance
- Applied Faith
- Going the Extra Mile
- Pleasing Personality
- Personal Initiative
- Positive Mental Attitude
- Enthusiasm
- Self-Discipline
- Accurate Thinking
- Controlled Attention
- Teamwork
- Adversity & Defeat
- Creative Vision
- Health
- Budgeting Time & Money

➢ Habits

In reading Napoleon Hill's work, at first, I have to be honest when I first read the copy of Think and Grow Rich I had to re-read it and listen to the audio for it to make sense. A friend suggested that I read a similar version of Hill, "Grow Rich With Peace of Mind" and then the light bulb finally clicked. From there I read the other works of Hill "Keys to Success" and "Outwitting the Devil". I felt like I was not only implementing these success principles before I even knew about Hill's work but it really felt surreal when it came to life. I was honored to meet Sharon Lecter herself who annotated Outwitting the Devil and have interviewed her on a few of my radio shows. I met Berny Dorhmann who had the privilege of having Hill around as his mentor. I had Don Green (CEO of The Napoleon Hill Foundation) put in his personal testimony on my best-seller You Are Not Alone and had JB Hill (grandson of Hill) autograph my Think and Grow Rich book. I also have a 1st Edition copy of Think and Grow Rich!

What fascinated me most about Hill's work is how his work continues to live on today as his legacy. I see people from different walks of life reading Think and Grow Rich and how it has changed their lives. It did make me wonder however what was the difference in people. Why is it that some read the book and succeed while others read and re-read the book but do not succeed?

I observed two things; first, people forgot the word "Grow" in the title and just focused on "Think" as if sitting and meditating on a vision board was enough to obtain success or riches. Grow means to take action and endure, to persevere through those challenges.

Second, it has to do with your vibrational frequency, meaning you have to be in alignment. Yes, starting with your thoughts helps align your frequency but everything else accounts and matters including your habits, your choices, your lifestyle, your health, and removing the energetic blockages of hurts, habits and hiccups.

When I was asked to lead this book project, I looked at a wall in my house, which has all 17 scrolls of Hill's principles and picked my favorites:

- ➢ Applied Faith
- ➢ Definiteness of Purpose
- ➢ Adversity & Defeat
- ➢ Positive Mental Attitude

Since I was not going to write an entire book on all of my favorites, I decided to write about applied faith because that was the determining factoring I saw in common with many of the women in this book project. All of us have a level of fear somewhere in life but it was faith that took fear's place that allowed courage and perseverance to take place. I call this, "Your faith has to be greater than your fear", it is almost like your secret weapon. You can know your purpose until your mind is swelling with positive thoughts and encounter every adversity but it is the hidden faith that magically appears to get through the fear.

You first have to believe to see, not see to believe---that is faith. Faith is also being ok with the outcome of a situation even if you envisioned it differently. For example, when I moved to a new city with my two small children, I had this feeling and knowing that I was supposed to move. With faith I could not 'see' certain things or anything at all; like "how". How was I supposed to provide income for my family while at the same time restarting both my businesses? How was I supposed to get help with 2-kids being a single parent and there was nobody I knew in this new city, no family, no friends. "How, this, how that", all came to mind. When I set a goal or my mind on an intention and the results were not completely what I had pictured, I had to be ok with the outcome and not blame my faith, 'Well I should not have moved here because I thought it was going to look like this according to my plans..." Having faith is trusting the process of the journey, and yes we make mistakes along the way that we learn from.

With this one example, had I not moved to a new city because of all my fears, both my businesses would not have expanded globally and have the trajectory they are on now. I would not have grown spiritually and healed emotionally.

Your faith has to be greater than your fear it is one of the key secrets to the alchemy of adversity. There are beautiful blessings in the boulders of adversity.

Faith may be blind but what people do not realize is that faith does reveal itself eventually. It could be small whispers from a stranger or a confirmation of something that you hear or read. As a clue, there will be times when you must walk and put on the invisible cloak of faith itself; walking completely blind with no confirmations, whispers or validations…this is when you know your capacity has increased to fully trust faith itself.

Get inspired, uplifted and empowered. Find the real wonder woman within you and stand in the divinity of your truth.
-April Joy Ford

BIO

April Joy Ford turns her tragedies into triumph by writing, speaking and teaching on how to overcome trauma and women's advocacy.

After being an Engineer for over 13 yrs at Intel, she realized that her faith was greater than her fear and walked away to become a Best-Selling Author, Speaker-Radio Host, and Motivational Coach.

Being a survivor of childhood sexual abuse and becoming a widowed single parent at only 32, April's tragedies gave her the opportunity to hit the reset button on life to discover who she was truly meant to be. She teaches others how to do the same.

Her best-sellers are: "You Are Not Alone- How to Rise Above Life's Challenges", "Journeys To Success – Women's Edition" and "Chase the Challenge and Conquer." She's been featured on National & Int'l media including her holistic training program "Breakthrough The Barriers- using the 4 Steps". This training program is being utilized to teach staff and survivors in group homes on trauma informed care and self-care.

As the host of a weekly live global show "You Are Not Alone" with VoiceAmerica Empowerment, April Joy has been able to provide her media platform for others to share their message of inspiration and empowerment and be there own voice. Each listener is a life and each life matters. Listeners globally tune in seeking answers and solutions to their situations and setbacks. The show's focus is to provide tools, tips and techniques holistically to overcome adversity.

Her brand, J.O.Y. started the vision of how we can rise above life's challenges to discover who we're truly meant to be and to share and spread our joys & blessings.

Her dedication expanded to a non-profit, Joy's G.I.F.T. (Global Illumination Foundation Thrives) empowering survivors from loss or sexual abuse by providing them with wrap around resources and services focused on mental, emotional, physical and spiritual healing. Survivors learn coping skills to recover from trauma and life skills for restoration of self-mastery of independence.

April Joy's gift to you is a survival guide to life's challenges from her best seller "You Are Not Alone – How To Rise Above Life's Challenges"

www.myjoyagain.com

To follow her work: www.joysofyah.com

INTRODUCTION
By: Tom "too tall" Cunningham

Welcome to volume 3 in the Journeys To Success: Empowering Stories Inspired by The Success Principles of Napoleon Hill book series. As the creator and producer of Journeys To Success, I am blessed beyond measure to become friends with the authors in these books. Learning about their personal journey, including their failures, mistakes and challenges has filled my heart, soul and mind in many positive ways and I know they will do the same for you.

This volume is dedicated to Women's Stories and I am very proud to have collaborated with the incredible April Joy Ford for this book. April and I chose authors who are pursuing their purpose with passion and were willing to share the struggles and challenges they faced along the way. You will be deeply touched emotionally as you read the book, and our authors truly hope that you connect with them personally to assist you in any way they can. They want to be your encourager as you positively pursue your own specific life's purpose and serve others to make this world a better place to live.

Napoleon Hill wrote extensively about women in all his books including Law of Success and Think and Grow Rich. I imagine that when the book was published in 1937, women were likely not considered equal to men in the pursuit of wealth, success and a life purpose. It is commendable that Hill saw the potential for the 17 Principles of Success to be used by both women and men equally. In his writings, Napoleon Hill also wrote in detail about the life-changing blessing of having your spouse as your mastermind partner.

My God given life's purpose is to encourage people to live positively with and through the many and varied challenges of life. The Journeys To Success book series serves that purpose very well.

This book would not have been possible without three very positive, talented and successful people that I am blessed to call friends.

When I first thought about a volume dedicated to women's stories I immediately thought of April Ford to lead the team. I met April at the Think and Grow Rich Summit in Del Mar, CA about 4 years ago. For 3 days, April, Tom Sutter, and I sat at the same table and got to know each other well. We discussed our purposes, goals, lives and passions. April's story of losing her young husband to a tragic death and being a single mother with two small children touched my soul. Please connect personally with April on social media. You will be glad you did.

My Publisher, John Westley Clayton, exemplifies one of Andrew Carnegie's favorite success principles; Going The Extra Mile. The number of edit and change requests that John Westley receives from the co-authors are quite significant. Formatting a book is not easy. Not only do you need the skill and talent to do it, you also need the patience to keep up with all the content and requests. If you are considering writing and self-publishing a book, I HIGHLY recommend that you contact John Westley. He can teach you what needs to be done and he will also publish your book for you.

The real reason that Journeys To Success: Napoleon Hill Inspired Stories became a series of books is because of Brad Szollose. Brad was one of the authors from volume 1 and, as we were working on the cover, he told me that he thought I had come up with an amazing idea that could be a great series of books. I clearly remember sitting back in my home office chair after he told me that and thinking to myself; "Brad is right. People have great stories to share and Napoleon Hill's Success Principles are used by everyone to some degree or another, whether they knew it or not". Thank you Brad for planting that thought into my consciousness. Brad also creates all the front and back covers in the Journeys To Success series. I have received MANY compliments about the covers and I love to just stare at them on my bookshelves. Brad's covers are eye catching, unique and inspiring.

If you would like to contribute a chapter to one of the upcoming volumes, please contact me. It will serve my purpose to share your Journey To Success with the world.

Tom "too tall" Cunningham

Napoleon Hill Foundation Certified Instructor

Creator of the Journeys To Success book series

Founder of Journey To Success Radio

www.tom2tall.com

MY MARRIAGE WITH FOOD AND FITNESS
By: Therese Cote

"Our only limitations are those we set up in our own minds."
– Napoleon Hill

I was very fortunate in my younger years to have a slender build and to be able to eat whatever I wanted without getting fat. Those were the days! I always had a very good appetite. People would ask me where all the food was going and I would just shrug my shoulders. I had no answer. I was just grateful it was not parking at my waistline! In my twenties, I gave birth and my post-pregnancy weight was less than my pre-pregnancy weight and yes, I wore my jeans out of the hospital. I was most comfortable with my weight and body when I was in my thirties. I had gained 5 to 8 pounds, but my small frame carried itself very well. Things changed quite a bit in my forties. My weight had slowly and gradually inched its way to an uncomfortable and undesirable extra 25 pounds. That is a lot for someone who had always been very slender. What happened? How did I get that way? I never had to worry about weight my entire life and then I found myself suddenly hiding behind clothes because I felt ashamed, powerless, very unhappy and depressed.

What I did not tell you is that I was always an emotional eater. I was suffering inside for a very long time. I experienced a traumatic event when I was 5 years old and I did not know how to release my feelings so food became my comfort throughout my life. I used it to feed my emotions, both good and bad. I was depressed, so I ate. I was sad, so I ate. To celebrating something, I ate. When I hung out with friends, I ate. When I was bored, I ate. Never-ending. I also used food as a way to punish myself. I believed that somehow that incident was my fault. I hated myself and hated my body so if I kept eating foods that made me feel good I could somehow 'distort' the way I looked (by getting fat) and felt (mmm.... pop, chips and chocolate). I had no idea I had this destructive behaviour but I did it for years. Well, I was not experiencing the negative emotions I mentioned earlier because of the weight gain. I was feeling this way because I came head to head with the REAL cause of my eating! I might have been able to hide the fat behind the clothes but my emotions were raw and exposed. The good news is that I recognized it was time for some self-care. I needed to do something, and fast! My self-worth and purpose were explored inside and out. The support I received involving the incident when I was five came late, but it was just what I needed. I faced my real problem. To regain power and control, I made a vow to myself. I was going to get into the best physical and mental shape of my life. I deserve that. I vowed to give myself that kind of love and care. It was my life and I owed it to myself to be the best I could be for ME. Nobody and nothing other than me could make that choice.

I was very eager to get started. It felt overwhelming at first but I had to act on it. My first action was joining a gym. I knew I needed structure and discipline and to be accountable, so along with a membership I made a one year commitment with my own personal trainer. I gave myself one year to make changes that would last. It was the absolute BEST decision and gift to myself! It was expensive but I sacrificed other things to make my health a priority. Honestly, it was worth every single dollar! In Think and Grow Rich, Napoleon Hill wrote that, "The ease with which lack of persistence may be conquered will depend entirely upon the intensity of one's desire. The starting point of all achievement is DESIRE." My desire was strong and showing up for my training sessions was the easy part because I was paying good money and if I wanted results I had to show up. There was a lot of sweat and tears during this process but with persistence and perseverance I pushed through the physical pain, exhaustion, and emotions that accompanied my transformation. It was very emotional as well. I kept asking myself, "Can I do this?" "Am I too old for this?" "Is my goal unrealistic?" It was the first time I felt empowered. The beginning of training is brutal because your body is not used to being pushed beyond its limits. But over time, and with much encouragement and support from my trainer, I got comfortable with the after-burn and my endurance had improved significantly. I loved the sweat. I had to literally peel my gym clothes off of me. I could hear my trainer's voice inside my head telling me the sweat was my fat crying so it was an honour to be sweaty! Changes started happening. I was sleeping better and was much more awake and alert during the day. I was also more efficient and managed stress much better. My confidence also soared. And guess what? I did not crave bad food any longer! As I started to feel stronger physically and mentally, I chose no to put processed food in my body. I found it easy to make healthier choices. I had become very disciplined in the grocery store and I had no desire to cheat myself of optimal health. I actually enjoy cooking. People would challenge me at work or social gatherings and say, "Come on, have some. You can afford it. You will burn it off easy." It was at these times that I was reminded of something else I had read in Think and Grow Rich which stated that "Close friends and relatives, while not meaning to do so, often handicap one through 'opinions' and sometimes through ridicule, which is meant to be humorous." Isn't it interesting how others can make excuses for us? I was proud of myself for declining all temptations.

I felt no urges to cheat and I started noticing how uncomfortable other people became when I ate with them. I did not preach to anyone, unless they asked or wanted to know about my journey. Mostly, I was happy. People in the gym were inspired by me and kept complimenting me and I felt like there was nothing I could not achieve in life. I worked hard and stayed committed to attending my sessions. Along the way, my trainer had become one of my dearest friends. He took this journey with me and I am forever grateful for him being there for me every step of the way. Training is very empowering. By the end of year one, I was pleased with what I had achieved but I felt I could still do more. I set a new goal. I made another one-year commitment with my trainer. My life had changed so much in one year. My gym bag became my purse and I never left home without it. I could not imagine not going to the gym. It was an amazing feeling. Over time I had established an amazing collection of workout gear and I rewarded myself with form-fitting attire. I did not start out that way. I did not have the confidence to wear anything that hugged my body. Now I was free. I did not need to hide behind food or clothing any longer. I had achieved my goal.

My diet was consistent with my workouts. I took my training seriously. I pre-planned my meals and weighed out everything to ensure the proper portion sizes. Grocery shopping became quite enjoyable because, when you eat clean, you only need to shop the perimeter of the grocery store. With the exception of tuna and a few miscellaneous items, those middle aisles are the processed and unhealthy aisles. I felt no desire to cruise down those aisles. I was able to shop quickly and easily. I would say my biggest challenge with food was keeping my meals interesting. In hindsight, I may have restricted my diet a little too much. I should have allowed for more options. I threw out all my condiments so I relied on herbs and spices for flavour and I steam cooked everything. I felt satisfied after I ate and not full because that was all my body required. I was eating for survival, not to meet any other needs. I was free from my bad association with food and entered a marriage of food and fitness for optimal health. It felt amazing! Those were my best years! I was so proud of myself for all that I had accomplished. It was the first time I did not mind being photographed. Before then, I never liked photos of myself.

Year two with my trainer was ending it was an emotional time for me. He has been a positive influence on my life and had been my rock as I fought my way through my barriers. It was challenging and hard work, I won't lie about that. I was fortunate enough to have a good partnership with my trainer. I saw him consistently three times a week over two years so part of me was sad to have our professional relationship end. I did not want it to be over. But two years had come to an end. The 'training wheels' had to come off and I needed to fly on my own. During that time, I was faced with crises in my life. At work, we were getting ready to move into a new building and I was reassigned to a different unit within the organization once the move occurred. I was not happy about that, and it was a major change for me. I had to adapt to working with a completely new team in a new building with new operating systems. My father had also been diagnosed with a very rare form of cancer. It was aggressive and there was no treatment for it. Surgery was not an option. It was their professional opinion that he would die within months. I was his Power of Attorney so I had to be on-call and face some difficult decisions along the way. My father lived out of town. He needed me. My family needed me. My employer needed me. My life was not about me any longer; it was about others needing me. I made the decision to go home to take care of my dad. I had a rather abrupt ending with my trainer but he understood that I needed to go.

It was the right choice for me to go home. I am happy I got to spend the time I did with my father because he did not live long. He died within four months. Those months felt like a lifetime. His funeral was the day before my birthday. Everything happened so fast. I have to tell you about my dad. My dad was full of life and energy. He and my mom separated when I was around twelve years old but they have remained friends and lived in the same city. He lived in an apartment complex for the elderly and he was quite the social butterfly. He remained active after his retirement. He would go out and shovel the parking lot of his complex in the cold northern winter so people could park. He always needed to be doing something. He would help them decorate the community centre for the dances and events they hosted in their building. He loved to dance and was also quite the pool shark. People learned never to bet money on a game of pool with my dad. They knew they would lose! He cruised around on his moped. He loved being around people, and he loved his family. He loved every single holiday and celebrated like he was a five year old. I watched him suffer and I mean, he suffered; yet in his darkest hours he never once complained. He had a few angry outbursts because he was not ready to die and the cancer was winning but he never complained. I watched my father deteriorate to 55 pounds in a very short time. He sometimes asked me to help him out of bed so he could shave and comb his hair but I would not let him. It was not safe for him to get out of bed and I did not want him looking at himself in the mirror. Maybe that was selfish of me. He really cared about how he looked and I did not want him to be focussed on that. We made sure dad looked good. I stopped caring for me when I started caring for dad. I was not at the gym. I was sitting in a hospital. My diet was pretty much non-existent. I found it difficult to eat under such stress and allowed my emotions to take over my own well-being. After dad's funeral, I was numbed by the aftermath. I had to empty his apartment, pay his bills and decide who was getting what. It was over-whelming. I came home and had to find some normalcy in my life again.

This was a dark and difficult time for me. My emotions were trying to catch up with the events. When I got to sit quietly with my own thoughts, I started questioning my purpose again. I questioned everything I worked so hard for at the gym. Why did it matter when cancer can take anyone at any time? I was grieving and exhausted and I needed to make sense of dad's passing. Here was this strong and active man who was gone in a matter of months. I had a lot of negative self-talk going on in my head. My demons were back; the same ones that drove me to comfort eating. My training was over. I did not have that support any longer. Unfortunately, I returned to food to soothe my emotions. Any and all food. And in greater quantities than ever! My visits to the gym became more sporadic and eventually I cancelled my membership. All that hard work had no significant meaning anymore. I felt like a failure in a big way. At 47 years old, I achieved my fitness goal of 127 pounds and 15% total body fat. That was amazing! How could I let it all go? Two years of hard work, gone! This setback really hit me hard. I was angry and confused about what really matters in life. My body went through yet some more changes and I was back at the starting line again.

> *"When defeat comes, accept it as a signal that your plans are not sound, rebuild those plans, and set sail once more toward your coveted goal"*
> *– Napoleon Hill*

I went through an emotional time. My body and mind got off track but one thing that had not changed was my resilience. My spirit was not broken. The way I look at fitness and food is somewhat different than before. The majority of your success lies in what you put in your mouth so I spent more time focused on that first. I wanted to get this right once and for all. I choose to eat clean, whole foods. I also discovered a Canadian company who makes their own healthy spice blends which enable you to make your own sauces, dips, rubs, salad dressings, condiments and so on. It makes cooking fun, time-efficient and delicious. It is easier to enjoy clean eating. Along with that, I took a nutrition-coaching program to help keep me on track and have a greater understanding. In fact, I am now offering online nutrition coaching and I am very excited about helping others. My motto is, "don't let your mood choose your food" for all those emotional eaters out there. My program offers guidance and support for one full year. During that time, you will be able to adopt and implement habit-based behaviours and have a better understanding of the psychology of food. This is not a diet. You will just eat smart and choose foods wisely. If you commit to this program, you will achieve your personal goal. I am not a model, television personality or personal trainer. I do not get endorsements to sell anyone anything. I am a role model for others who have been suffering like I had. I am also a nurse with a wealth of knowledge and personal experience that I can share with authenticity. I have found a renewed purpose, and it feels wonderful! My journey continues.

As far as exercise, I know I am capable of following structured fitness, so I signed up for high intensity 30 minute classes. These workouts are very intense and use your entire body. They kick your cardio in the pants and I sweat just as much, if not more than when I was weight lifting. I can attend 7 days a week for half an hour each time. This is attainable. I am not spending hours at the gym like I used to which is perfect for my current lifestyle. I am not saying not to do this, but I have many more commitments than I had before. I always did a warm-up, then my training session, then a cool-down including stretching and then showered. It was easy to spend a few hours in the gym that way. It worked for me then. Any activity or movement is good for your body. You just have to commit to doing it. Plan the time and do it. As I go through my current transformation, I always feel great immediately after the gym. I am much more forgiving to myself and I laugh at myself more. People tell me about this so called 'muscle memory' I am supposed to have since working out previously. Well, I'm not so sure where that went. My muscle memory must have Alzheimer's because I am not experiencing the same endurance I once had. I will get there again and I continue to challenge myself.

My life is happy and peaceful. I have much to give to the universe. I forgive myself, love myself more, and have learned from every hurdle I have jumped. My strength comes from within. I will keep moving forward. I rely on my loved ones for support and unconditional love instead of food. What I get from that is much more significant and satisfying. My pain is now my gift. I have a healthy marriage with fitness and food and use it to inspire others. I am blessed to have a wonderful life and I express gratitude for it every single day.

BIO

Therese Cote is an Amazon International Bestselling co-author of Journeys to Success: 21 Empowering Stories Inspired by the Success Principles of Napoleon Hill, Volume One. Her success with the first book has inspired her to continue following her passion for writing. This is one of her proudest accomplishments.

Therese has an abundance of experience in Healthcare. She works as a Nurse, specializing in Forensic Psychiatry. This challenging role primarily focuses on Risk Management and reintegration into society. She advocates to bring awareness about suicide and to reduce stigma associated with mental health.

In addition, she is also a Nutrition Coach. She has received her certification through Precision Nutrition. She offers her clients online coaching, mentorship and support for a clean eating lifestyle. The program is designed to help clients understand their eating habits, psychology of food and making the necessary changes to meet their nutritional and weight goals. The results are sustainable and life-changing as the program is offered for one full year. To learn more about her services, go to http://www.care4yourlife.ca or to learn more about

Precision Nutrition, go to http://www.precisionnutrition.com and follow them on social media for a variety of interesting articles, news and updates.

She is dedicated to her family and strives for a good work/life balance. Her blended family brings her a tremendous amount of pride and joy. Understanding the frailty of mental health, she actively seeks out activities that provide self-care such as exercise, meditation, reading, music, massages, going to a spa, and one of her favourites is connecting with nature. The elements of the earth keep her grounded and allow her to continue giving to others in all the ways she has dedicated her life to doing.

NOT EVERYONE CHARGED WITH A CRIME IS GUILTY
By: Kim Cunningham

"No person can succeed in a line of endeavor which one does not like"
– Napoleon Hill.

"You can start right where you stand and apply the habit of going the extra mile by rendering more service and better service than you are now being paid for"
– Napoleon Hill

Many, if not most, people assume that if a person is charged with a crime then they are likely guilty of the charge. Working as a law clerk for a criminal defense lawyer taught me different.

At the age of 24 I became a single mom and was not receiving any child support. I needed to go to college and find an industry and job where I could support my son and myself and decided to become a paralegal or law clerk.

I went to school for six hours each weekday for one year and also worked four hours each day in a lawyer's office practicing what I had learned at school. Anyone who has worked part-time while going to college while being a single parent to a young child knows how challenging that is.

When I graduated I immediately had 3 job offers and accepted one with a family law lawyer in Toronto. I spent a few years commuting to that job, working on divorces and child support matters mostly. Family law is difficult because your own clients may lie to you and hide their assets from their spouse. In many divorces the clients express hatred of their spouse. I try to remind people that they once did love their spouse. Working with angry clients who may be lying to you can be stressful. To work in family law, you need to be emotionally strong, otherwise you could be sucked into the emotional turmoil of your clients and take that stress home to your family. The good part about family law is that there are many people who have been treated cruelly and unfairly, and sometimes even criminally, during the marriage that I was able to help. Many times a family law matter turns into a criminal matter when one spouse makes an allegation to the police in order to gain leverage in their family law matter. Overall, the relief and peace of mind of our clients after their divorce made me feel good about having a small part to play in their positive life change.

For the most part I enjoyed my work, however, I had a boss who was, to be kind, not a good boss or a positive person. I will not go into details about his behaviour but it was clear to me that I had to find another job. A friend of mine who knew I was looking to move onto something new, phoned me to let me know that a lawyer had just moved into their building and she was looking for a law clerk. I told her I was interested and my friend gave her my resume and told her about me. I went for the interview and met Sharon Ingle, probably the most amazing person I have ever met. I was truly blessed to work for her for 9 years and we also became great friends. She hired me on the spot.

Sharon was a criminal defense lawyer and on my first day of work she brought me to the courthouse for a case she was working on. She addressed the Justice of the Peace and Crown Attorney briefly about a few matters and then scheduled the next court date. When we left the courtroom Sharon said to me, "Did you see how I did that?" I said, "Yes" and she said, "Wonderful that is now part of your job". From that day forward I would be required to attend court to appear on her behalf. I would be speaking to Judges, Justices' of the Peace, and Crown Attorney's to adjourn cases, set Trial dates, schedule Judicial Pre-Trials and conducting resolution meetings with Crown Attorneys. I was terrified when I learned this. Public speaking is rated as the most fearful thing a person could do and I was definitely in that category. For the first few months Sharon had to tell me exactly what to say and I would write it on cue cards and read them. Each cue card started with 'My name is…' because I thought I would be so nervous that I would forget my name. After 2 or 3 months I mastered the job and ditched the cue cards, although as Sharon was the lawyer and the person in charge, she provided me with instructions on what needed to be done in court. I got to know all the crown attorneys, judges, justices of the peace, court clerks and court officers because we had a lot of clients and I was in the courthouse every day for several hours.

The nine years I worked for Sharon Ingle were by far the best 9 working years of my life. She was a great boss, which initially I had worried about because I had thought that I would not like working for a woman. We often said we expected to be rolling our briefcases through the courthouse in our 90's and never wanted to retire. People in the courthouse called us the Dynamic Duo. Not only was she a great boss, Sharon was also a great and very highly respected lawyer and friend. Sharon was such a smart and brilliant person that she would have done well and earned a lot of money in any field of law. She decided on criminal law and initially was a partner in a law firm, but later on decided that she would prefer to work for herself so that she could live the lifestyle she loved, which involved a lot of sports. Sharon was on the Canadian tennis team and was also a triathlete. She would ride her bicycle to work and change her clothes when she got to the courthouse. Because I got so proficient at my job, she was able to spend a lot of time training for and participating in triathlons.

We had many interesting cases in the nine years we worked together, and I have chosen a few to share with you.

Bipolar Husband

One day while I was in the office a woman phoned. She was crying and asked if she could come to our office right away because she had been charged with assaulting her husband. I told her to come and see us. When she arrived she told us her story. She had been married for many years, had two teenage children and her husband was bipolar.

On the day in question she was at home with her daughter and husband when he erupted in anger. He was yelling and screaming at her and she became quite scared. She went to her daughter's room and stayed there with her. While they were there they heard a loud commotion in the house and went down the hallway to see what was happening. She and her daughter saw her husband banging his head against the headboard of their bed. He then proceeded to phone the police and tell them that his wife had assaulted him. When the police arrived he repeated his allegation to them and, despite the daughter crying and telling them that her father had inflicted the wounds on himself, they arrested our client and brought her to the jail. Because it was in the evening, and because anyone charged with assault requires a bail hearing, she was processed, including being strip searched, and spent the night in jail. This was a fifty-year-old woman who had never even had a parking ticket and here she was spending a night in jail.

Sharon told her that we were happy to help her and, although she would not believe it at the moment, that in 6 months she would thank her husband for what he did. After several negotiations with the crown attorney, it was agreed that our client would sign a Peace Bond for 12 months with conditions to keep the peace and be of good behavior and to not have any contact with her husband unless in the presence of her family law lawyer. She and her husband ended up getting divorced and, although her husband was bipolar, he was also a sharp businessperson, and so she ended up with a good amount of money. She got her own apartment and really felt at peace and grateful for what had happened to her. She told me that if it had not happened she would never have divorced her husband. Like Sharon had told her six months earlier, she was thankful that her husband did what he had done.

Phallometric testing

Sharon met with a client who had been charged with a sexual assault, inappropriate touching of a male child in an elevator. The client denied the allegations and Sharon could not tell if he was telling her the truth or not. She asked me to interview him to see what I thought.

I sat down with him in my office and, as I was speaking with him, I had formed the opinion that he had in fact committed a criminal offense and so I decided to give him my spin on phallometric testing. Phallometric testing is done using a penile plethysmograph, basically a lie detector for the penis. It measures the change in penis circumference in response to sexual and nonsexual stimuli. I told him that if he wanted to prove his innocence he would have to see a psychiatrist and have the test done to prove to the court that he was not a pedophile. I let him know that he would be hooked up and shown images of underage boys. I told him that if he became aroused it would send a strong jolt of electricity though his penis which would cause great pain and shoot him out of his seat. This was actually not quite the truth and but an embellishment of it. After my description he jumped up onto the chair and was prancing like a horse saying "ok I did it, I did it, don't make me take the test". I left the room and told Sharon he did it and he was not particularly interested in phallometric testing.

Girl wanting a kitten

One of our clients was a man who owned a pizza parlor and was living with a woman who had a six-year-old child. The girl would often climb into her mother and the man's bed in the middle of the night when she would wake up.

Our client was very allergic to cats and the little girl really wanted a kitten. The little girl saw her father every other weekend. The father and daughter were very close and spent lots of time bonding with each other. He told her that he would get her a kitten if she came to live with him. After that the girl the girl lied and told her mother that her boyfriend had touched her inappropriately. Police were called and our client was arrested. He strongly denied the charges and insisted on a trial to prove his innocence.

Sharon loved cats and had 3 of her own. She had the opportunity to question the girl on the stand. In a very soft voice Sharon talked to her about her cats, especially her favorite one who she called Slice. She showed the little girl a picture of Slice wearing a Santa hat. The little girl immediately told Sharon that she too loved cats. She said that her mom's boyfriend was very allergic to cats but that her daddy had told her that if she lived with him he would get her a kitten. That was the end of the story. The judge found our client not guilty.

Indecent act in public

One of our clients was charged with an indecent act. A family reported that he was naked in his car while they were in the parking lot of a provincial park. The family kept moving their car around the lot to see what our client was doing. They thought he was doing something illicit and phoned the police however our client was gone by the time they arrived.

The very next day the police went to the park again and found our client naked in his car reading a pornographic magazine. The police asked him why he was naked and he told them that he had needed to defecate and had done so in the nearby woods. He even showed them where he had done it. The police said that did not explain why he was naked in his car. He then told them that he was diabetic and so erections were few and far between and that he had needed to take care of one that had suddenly come up (pun intended). He was arrested and charged with an indecent act.

During his guilty plea his wife took the witness stand as she wanted to address the court. She gave a heartfelt rendition of their marriage and testified about her husband's diabetes, and their lack of a sex life. She then proceeded to sob and say, "I just can't believe he wasted one". Upon hearing this, the judge felt it was immediately necessary to stop the proceedings and go to his chamber in order to contain his amusement. The client was found him guilty of an indecent act and he received one-year probation with a condition not to attend any provincial park.

Abandoned child

Sharon and I represented a good number of young offenders and I learned that parents are often the reason why a child becomes a criminal. A fourteen-year-old boy who was charged with vandalism is an example of that. This boy had been caught breaking store windows at night and had been charged with Mischief Over $5,000.00. We found out that his parents were divorced. His mother did not want him to live with her and so his father was given sole custody. The father decided to live with his girlfriend at her place and so he rented a small apartment for his son. The father came by once a week to give our client $100 for groceries and spending money for the week. Other than that this youth had no contact with his parents. Like many kids seeking love and attention our client acted out and started his vandalism spree and was charged. Our client entered a guilty plea and a conviction was entered against him as a young offender and he was sentenced to 2 years of probation and counselling to address his issues.

Those are just a few of the many interesting cases I worked on during those nine years working with Sharon. Sharon and I would still be working together however she was diagnosed with cancer at the age of 49 and died 5 years later after a determined battle with the disease. At one point during her treatment, after six rounds of chemo, she brought home two bronze and one silver medal from the provincial Masters swimming championships in Ottawa. After the competition, one of her competitors told her that she was on fire in the pool. Sharon told her that she was feeling kind of sluggish as she had just completed her sixth round of chemotherapy. Her competitor could not believe that Sharon had beaten her and won after all she had gone through.

Because I spent so much time in the courthouse I became very friendly with all the Judges and Justices of the Peace. One time while in traffic court, when the Justice of the Peace entered the courtroom, he told the clerk to hold down the matter as he wanted to see my vacation photos.

Another time, the same Justice of the Peace told the court officer that he believed there was a warrant for my arrest and that the court officer should arrest me. When I protested, the court officer approached me, and the Justice of the Peace smiled and said "Officer I believe I may have been mistaken". Another time, while in court, after I had requested an adjournment of a matter, the Judge said, "That is all well and good but you could have just said nana nana poo poo".

I have learned after many years working as a law clerk that, even when I did not know it, I was making a positive difference in people's lives. Several years ago, while I was at a movie with my husband, a young man approached me to thank me for my guidance during his court matter and said that my advice had made an impact on him. He told me that he was now an upstanding citizen who was married with a child and owned his own business.

Napoleon Hill, in his book Think and Grow Rich, writes that having a Definite Purpose, or Definite Chief Aim in life is the starting point of all achievement. Without a purpose, plan, and goals most people end up as drifters in life. I have discovered that my purpose in life is to help other people with my legal skills, knowledge and experience. I have been able to help clients as well as be a valuable source of advice and money saving for friends and acquaintances. One of my favorite Napoleon Hill quotes is, "If you cannot do great things, do small things in a great way". That is how I feel about the work that I do for my clients as well as the friends and acquaintances I help. In a small way, I am using my legal skills, talents and experience to serve people and I love it.

BIO

Kim Cunningham has spent most of her career as a law clerk working in real estate, family and criminal law. She currently works in family law for Keith Elliott of the law firm O'Marra & Elliott in Port Credit, Ontario. She is a mother of 2 sons, Micheal (age 24) and Will (age 27) and mother-in-law to Jessica. She is also a grandmother to 3-year-old Helena. Helena calls her Yaya and loves spending time with her.

She was adopted by amazing parents, Marie and Ken, and had an ideal childhood. Sadly, her father died of cancer at the age of 51 when she was only 15 years old. Her mother Marie became a single parent and continued to provide a supportive home with lots of love. They have become inseparable and talk on the phone almost every day. Her mother is currently 91 years old, living on her own and driving. Marie is Kim's biggest fan and supporter.

Kim is married to Tom "too tall" Cunningham, creator of the Journeys To Success book series and a Napoleon Hill Foundation Certified Instructor. Tom is also the Founder of Journey To Success Radio on BlogTalkRadio.

Kim can be reached at mrstom2tall@gmail.com

MONEY TIPS FROM THE BAKER'S DAUGHTER
By: Chella Diaz

I was 8 years old and my dad told me that girls must have long hair. It did not make sense to me, so I went out raised the money and went to get a haircut. My dad was walking home and he had a basket on his head (he was a baker and carried the bread in the basket) and could not look down. He reached out to touch my head and immediately noticed I did not have my long ponytail. Looking back I can see what a strong personality I had and I did not believe in gender roles.

I was 9 and I was outside playing with a little black boy, I did not think anything of it. My mother yelled and screamed at me to get in the apartment. She told me I was to never ever again play with the little black boy. Years later I married an African American man.

I was in middle school and my dad had two full time jobs. One of the paychecks went into a savings account for a down payment on a house. It took him about 6 months to save the money, which felt like years to me. We could not play inside and could not make any noise because my dad was sleeping. They purchased a 3-bedroom house in Carson (what State?). We lived in Carson for 3 years and moved the summer before my senior year. They sold the house and purchased 6 units and he also ended up purchasing 5 other properties. I learned so much about how to manage money from my dad.

When I was 9 years old I went to a farmers market and knew which vendors had the lowest prices and highest quality. I purchased my car when I was 17 years old and my home at 23 years old.

I got married, had two sons and worked in the corporate world for 20 years. As part of my job, I reviewed over 30,000 Real Estate loan applications. I witnessed how people struggled to manage money regardless of how much money they made.

One of the applications was from a Doctor who made $250,000 a year but had no savings. He had a car loan and several credit cards and he was requesting cash to pay off some of his credit card balances. The loan was denied. Even though he earned $250,000 annually he did not quality for the loan. Another loan application was from a mechanic shop owner who made $110,000 a year. He had $50,000 in savings, his car was paid off and he had small balance on his credit card, which he paid off every month.

I believe it does not matter how much money you make but rather how much you keep that counts. I saw a pattern in how the rich saved their money and the poor spent their money. The rich believe in paying themselves first. I suggest you start a savings account for the older version of yourself. What type of lifestyle does the older version of you want to have? How much money is it going to take to live that lifestyle?

In February 2012 the company I worked for was closed. I knew I wanted to teach money management, and so my entrepreneurship journey began.

I started going to networking events and hanging out with business owners. I had 5 people recommend the book Think and Grow Rich to me. I read it but only grasped about 10% of the content. I read several other books and re-read Think and Grow Rich again. This time I followed some of the steps.

Going from employee to a business owner took time. As an employee (and I was an outstanding employee) is different from running your own business. When running your business you can work and work and work and the money does not usually appear right away. As a business owner you must do the activities that generate income, not the things that keep you busy. This was a big shift for me. I am working on this as we speak. I think about it constantly and I am a work in progress.

It was during the first two years of my business journey that I found out who my true friends were. I lost a few friends in the process. There was a time when I was due to receive a payment in 10 days however I needed to make some repairs to my rental property before then. A dear friend who was working part time had $360 in his pocket and gave me $300 no questions asked. On the other hand, a friend who makes over $200,000 would not lend me the money until I told her why I needed it, when I would pay it back, and how I managed to get myself into that situation. That changed our relationship. I knew I wanted to make a difference in the world by empowering students make educated financial decisions.

This was also the time when other friends and relatives wanted me to get a job. It was not easy keeping my positive outlook. I understand now that my friends and family did not want me to change. When I changed they were going to have to choose to change. Change can be a scary thing for some people. Change is where you get to find out if you will stay on track or quit. I believe this is the reason so many businesses do not succeed and why they quit during the struggle. They give up too soon not realizing that there is a lot of satisfaction in completing a project.

From Think and Grow Rich in the chapter about Desire.

1. "Fix in your mind the exact amount of money you desire. It is not sufficient merely to say, I want plenty of money. Be definite as to the amount."
2. "Determine exactly what you intend to give in return for the money you desire." (This was a difficult step for me because I empower high school students to make educated financial decisions and I thought there should be a long line of people waiting to give me money because I was doing something good for them.)
3. "Establish a definite date when you intend to posses the money you desire.". I kept moving the date and I kept making things more complicated than they needed t be. One of my coaches favorite phrases is "Humans complicate everything".
4. "Create a definite plan for carrying out your desire, and begin at once, whether you are ready or not, to put this plan into action". I put the plan into

action, however I wasted a lot of time and did not attend as many workshops and classes as I should have. The mind chatter can be strong and the stories I told myself were very creative and made sense to me. It took me a while to realize that I was putting on the brakes of my own success.

5. "Write out a clear, concise statement of the amount of money you intend to acquire. Name the time limit for its acquisition. State what you intend to give in return for the money, and describe clearly the plan through which you intend to accumulate it". I did not have a plan and I did not know how I was going to find the students to teach my money management program to. I started calling high schools but only about 1 in 10 called me back.

6. "Read your written statement aloud, twice daily once before retiring at night and once after rising in the morning". It took me a long time to memorize my statement and when I read it out loud I felt like a liar. At this point I started working with personal development coaches.

Fourth Step:

"Knowledge will not attract money unless it is organized and intelligently directed through practical plans of actions to the definite end of accumulation of money." I could not understand why people were not lined up to give me lots of money to share my knowledge. At the first workshop I did at my cousins home, she invited a few teenagers and offered them breakfast if they attended. After that a friend challenged me do a workshop at her school and that was the beginning of teaching money mastery. I did a few workshops and hoped my work would spread like wildfire and that I would have people calling me to share my program with their students. This taught me patience and clarity. Wishing for something is just not enough. I had to make a mental shift. I had to face the facts…actions without a plan is a waste of time. Action without a destination is a waste of energy. I started asking for help which was not an easy step for me. I experienced many different emotions including feeling like a failure. The negative chatter in my head was very strong including thinking that; "I cannot do the job on my own and "Who did I think I was to teach money management?" I did not have an inspiring story. How can a baker's daughter teach money management? This is where amazing coaches appeared in my life. I recorded the presentations and with some help from a dear friend I turned them into a book titled 'Money Boot Camp: Financial literacy for teens.

Fifth Step:

Imagination – It was not until recently that I started thinking of myself as having imagination and being creative. I lived in an excel spreadsheet and numbers made sense to me. Let me give you an example; when I went grocery shopping I could keep track of the cost of the items in my cart in my head. When paying bills I knew how much I needed to distribute to each account; mortgage, insurance, groceries, going out to eat, movies, etc. I am talking about doing the math without using a calculator because numbers just made sense. I did not see how numbers making sense was a form of imagination. If you do not think you have an imagination it is very difficult to use something you do not think you possess. We all have an imagination but it is like any other gift, we need to put them to use. What are your gifts? How do you express your gifts? Who are you empowering with your gifts?

Sixth Step:

Organized Planning – the crystallization of desire into action. Being part of a mastermind or support system. I joined a few mastermind groups where people did not complete the tasks they said they would. It also felt like we were not lifting each other up. Some of the people wanted to socialize and complain. I got tired of hearing excuses and stopped participating. I am happy to report that I am currently part of one amazing mastermind group and I have two accountability partners. My suggestion is to find people that are going to support you and lift you up when you need it. All members must be committed to their success as well as the success of everyone in the group. Make a written contract so that everyone knows the rules and responsibilities. Set a time frame stating how long are you going to part of the mastermind because this allows everyone to see if they are willing to commit to the group.

Planning the sale of services was an eye opener for me. I knew the services I could deliver however I wondered why people should believe me. I started collecting written and video testimonials and I shared the testimonials. The biggest lesson I learned was not taking things personally. If people were not calling me back I was grateful for the experience and called another school, after school program or women's group. Initially, when I started sharing my expertise, I only went after schools, then one of my mentors suggested I look for opportunities in other areas such as after-school programs, foster care systems, and women's groups. The minute she opened my mind to new options I was asked to speak at an after school program. This is why I am so passionate about speaking to students about opening their minds to new options.

I never gave up even though it was not always easy. Stepping outside my comfort zone is where my journey began. I was asked to be on several podcasts and people started reaching out to me. I was put on several grant applications to teach money management to high school students.

Are you tired of working your fingers to the bone, and not having time to spend with your loved ones? Do you feel you are only working to keep up with your monthly bills and that there just is not enough money left over?

I know what it is like to feel pulled in a million directions, to feel guilty for working such long hours but at the same being trapped into that pattern by need.

After my divorce I had to start from scratch. All I had were my clothes and two boys to take care of. I purchased my home within 6 moths and I started a new job. I then realized I was working over 60 hours a week and was not spending time with my sons or my friends and that took a toll on me mentally and physically. I went back to basics and started to keep track of how I was spending my money. I was shocked to find where it was all going. I realized that with just a few tweaks, I could radically shift how much money was going out so that I would not need to work so har

Seventh Step:
The Mastery of Procrastination –This step took on many different forms. I would volunteer, offer to help others, go to workshops, attend networking events,

basically doing anything to keep myself busy so that I would not have to make a decision to work on my business. Keeping myself busy gave me an excuse as to why I could not make the calls I needed to make to move my business forward. Now it is easier for me to stay on track. I recommend that you make a list of people you need to contact to grow your business the night before. Making a list the night before, so that in the morning I take action, helped me to be more productive.

In a poll conducted by Citigroup of women over the age of 40, the following conclusions were made:

• Women carry balances on their credit card accounts. 60 percent of women said they carried a balance from one month to the next compared to 51 percent of men.

• Women pay only the minimum payment due. According to a recent study, 42 percent of women make a habit of paying only the minimum payment on their credit card accounts, compared to 38 percent of men.

• Women pay higher interest rates on credit cards. When it comes to looking for a new card, just 31 percent of women go rate shopping to get the best deal on a credit card. As a consequence, women pay more in interest than men.

• Women cannot resist a sale. According to a study published in the Journal of Financial Planning, 23.7 percent of women and only 4.5 percent of men agree they cannot resist a sale.

• Women buy more unplanned items. Noted in that same study, twice as many women as men agreed they buy unplanned items and buy without any true need. Women spend more on impulse.

It has never been more important to get control of your finances. With retirement security no longer a guarantee, the time to change our patterns is now!

I would like to share with you how I took control of my debt in just three easy steps and in turn, had more time to spend with my family and friends.

- 3 Keys to Master Your
- Money Skills
- Keep track of how you spend your money
- Divide what you spent into two lists
- Make a list of all your monthly obligations.

TRACKING

For one week keep track of your spending. Anytime you spend over $1.00 write it down. It is important that you keep track of how you are spending your money so that you can find out where your money holes are.

Suzy, one of my clients, followed the above task and was SHOCKED to find out that she was spending $1,200.00 a month on dining out. Armed with this knowledge she simply made a choice that would benefit her in the long run. She decided to start saving $700.00 a month towards paying off her credit card debt while reducing the amount spent eating out to $500.00. That simple shift changed her financial situation tremendously.

DIVIDE

Divide the money you spend into two lists. The first are your "Wants" and the other is your "Needs." How much did you spend in each category? This is where the magic happens and you begin to see where you can make different choices in your spending.

My client Pat liked to use the 24 to 72-hour cool off period. If there was something she wanted to buy she would wait 24 to 72 hours. If after the cool off period she still wanted the item she would get it. When she first started this practice, she would buy the item 80% of the time however, after 2 months the ratio dropped to 40%. This decrease made a huge difference in her disposable monthly income.

Maggie, another client, always went shopping when she was stressed. It was almost as if she created stressful situations to give her an excuse to shop!

With Maggie, what worked was the decision to choose three accountability partners. Before she made a purchase, she was required (according to our plan) to talk to one of her accountability partners. She chose 3 friends that she could call on before making a purchase. That way, if she could not get a hold of one of the partners she had two more to call to walk her through the temptation.

I have used this practice myself as well! Purchasing items on sale and buying personal development products are my weaknesses. I have 3 accountability partners who have been with me for over 5 years. I do not call on them as often now however it is good to know they are there should I need them to talk me out of something!

Of course, we want to set aside some "fun" money. Life is meant to be enjoyed! The imbalance occurs when we are spending more money each month on things like treats, home accessories, dinners out etc., than we are on paying towards our credit card debt!

THE BOTTOM LINE

Make a list of your monthly obligations, including the items that you pay on a quarterly or semi-annual basis. This is going to show you how much of your income you need to cover your obligations. For the items that are due quarterly or semi-annually, you will be able to prepare in advance.

77% of women have an average of $9,000.00 in credit card debt. They are stuck on a hamster wheel and do not know how to get out. They are making the credit card companies very rich. Tracking, dividing and staying on top of your obligations will allow you to put the interest you are paying to the credit card companies into your savings account instead!

You will always be one step ahead of your bills and you will know exactly how much you have left over to allocate to fun!

Ready to take charge?

By now I hope you see how keeping track of your spending, along with making a list of your monthly obligations is going to show you where your money goes and what new choices you can make. It is not always comfortable to take a hard look at our habits, but temporary discomfort is imperative for life long financial stability.

When you follow these three simple steps, you will be armed with the knowledge you need to form better spending habits and in doing so, will be able to work less and live more!

Bonus tips;

• What if you start savings for things such as vacations, school supplies, auto repairs etc. Each month you save toward the above items, you will always be ahead of the game. You will not fall into the catch-up trap. When the items show up you will be prepared to pay for them.

• Organize a clothes swap, imagine going home with several new outfits for the cost of the clothes sitting in your closet.

• Payoff your credit cards – stop making the credit card companies rich with all the interest you are paying them.

• Start a reserve account. Small steps toward this goal are better then no steps.

• Separate your money into 3 buckets; 1. Needs 2. Wants 3. Savings. There is only one rule; the buckets do not get to borrow from each other.

Quick recap 3 steps to setting a solid financial foundation:

1. Keep track of how you spend your money

2.Divide what you spend one into two list "Wants" and "Needs"

3.Make a list of all your monthly obligations

If you are having a bad day, go out and help someone else.

Hang out with people that are going to lift you up!!!

I believe it does not matter how much money you make …it is how much you keep that counts.

BIO:

Chella is an author, speaker, and money mastery coach. She has been a money magnet since she was a teenager! She purchased her own car at 17 and her house when she was 23 years old. She spent over 20 years in the lending industry and reviewed over 30,000 Real Estate Loan Applications. She noticed a pattern between how the wealthy saved their money and how the poor spent their money. It is her mission to help people keep more of their hard earned money while enjoying their time with loved ones.

She can be reached at Chella@moneyiq901.com

www.moneyIQ901.com

ANOTHER LEAP OF FAITH
By: Kat Downey

It was not until a few years ago, when I first read Napoleon Hill's book "Think and Grow Rich" that I realized I was implementing many of his principles, namely: Desire, Faith, Auto-Suggestion, Specialized Knowledge, Imagination, Organized Planning, Decision Making, and Persistence.

When I graduated from high school I knew that I wanted to go to university. I also knew that I did not want to take a Bachelor of Arts degree but rather a science degree. I enrolled in the Bachelor of Science degree in Human Kinetics. I had always dreamed of being a medical doctor, yet I did not think I was smart enough to do this. After graduating with a BSc.H.K., I applied to teacher's college and was accepted into the Intermediate and Senior Science and Physical Education stream.

One of the requirements of the program was to do a community placement throughout the year. I chose to teach mathematics and science, grades four to ten at a women's prison. Wow, was this an eye opener! Many of these women were not well educated and struggled academically. More often than not it was because they did not feel that they were worthy or capable of learning. This is likely the first time I recognized the relationship between self-esteem and academic achievement.

Graduating with a Bachelor of Education, I started off my professional educational career, teaching high school sciences: biology, chemistry, physics and physical education. I loved empowering the students to be confident of their academic success. Throughout this time the notion of traveling around the world was formulating in my mind. With this decision made and the planning in place, I approached my principal and told him I was quitting to travel around the world. With wise counsel, he suggested that I take a leave of absence rather than quit my position. His rationale was that you never know what could happen and I may need this position to return to. I chose to listen to him and did just that.

At the end of four years I took a leave of absence to travel around the world by bicycle, covering 6,000 km and seeing twelve different countries. During this time I had ample opportunity to enjoy the scenery of the world and contemplate what my next steps were. I loved teaching, yet high school was changing and I was not sure I wanted to continue in the high school system.

Arriving home after eleven months, broke and needing additional funds, I went to a nearby community college to see if there were teaching opportunities there. Fortunately they were in need of an instructor for the night school Prehealth Chemistry Program. This course was perfectly suited to me as I had taught chemistry at the high school level. The structure of this course was an academic review of the chemistry taught in high school so that the students were up to this grade level before entering health science programs the next semester.

Imagine my surprise and delight to be teaching adult students who wanted and needed to learn. They were totally motivated to succeed in this course. Yet often they shared with me their trepidation about learning chemistry. Many of the students had not been successful learning chemistry in high school and they were doubtful that they would be successful this time. Empowering their academic self-esteem was my primary focus. With a definite purpose in mind, I remember saying to these students that their job was to come to class, do what I asked them to do and they would "get" chemistry. A few weeks later you could see the pure joy in their faces that now they "got" chemistry and they were so thrilled to be able to do so.

During this night school course, the Chair of the Allied Health Sciences program contacted me and said "We like what you are doing here in the night school program, would you like to teach here full time?" How he knew this, I have no idea as I do not remember seeing him during the evening classes. I replied enthusiastically, absolutely, and he said "the Human Resources department is in this building and this is what you will need to take with you." Wow, I now had a full time academic position without an interview. I was ecstatic.

That fall, I started teaching in the Allied Health Science Division and loved what I was doing. Over the course of twelve years I taught thousands of students and thoroughly enjoyed the post-secondary academic setting. It was an absolute delight to teach students who were focused on achieving their diplomas in their selected academic programs. Over the course of teaching there for twelve years I had my three daughters; returning from maternity leave each time to continue teaching at the college.

As a lifelong learner, I upgraded my teaching qualifications and graduated with a Master of Education, specializing in Adult Education and Curriculum Design. One of the required courses was statistics. I remember the professor asking us to do an assignment following one particular method. I had been reading ahead in the textbook and felt that this assignment would be better managed doing a path analysis. I took a leap of faith and did the assignment following the path analysis route and explained my rationale for doing so. I submitted the assignment to the professor and a few days later he asked me to meet with him. I went into his office with trepidation and thought for sure I had failed that assignment. Rather he congratulated me and gave me a score of 12/10 for the assignment. I was elated and this was the first time I had academic confidence and felt that yes I was smart enough!

From the heights of graduating with honors on a Saturday and celebrating with family and friends, my world went to the depths of sorrow when I had a miscarriage on Sunday. I was devastated and understood grief and bereavement from a death perspective. It took some time before I could accept this and begin to understand that things happen for a reason. Another leap of faith.

Each time I returned from maternity leave, I noticed that my timing in the classroom was off and there were changes in the administrative procedures. Yet the third time I returned to teaching I sensed that something was different and I could not put my finger on it. I was totally focused on the course content and my student's academic success.

During this time I had an inkling to become a licensed Funeral Director. I do not remember when this idea first came into my head. Acting on this desire,

I phoned the college that offered this program to ask them how one became a licensed Funeral Director. It is hard to believe now, yet at this time there was no internet and one could not simply google something to find out information. Having chatted with the program coordinator for some time, I asked them if they would send me an application package in the mail.

One of the courses I was teaching was Oral Microbiology for Dental Hygienists. There were microbiology textbooks, but not one specifically for Dental Hygienists. I recognized this void and with definiteness of purpose I researched and wrote a manual specifically for Dental Hygienists.

One Tuesday at one o'clock p.m., I was asked to come down to the administration office. I did this readily, thinking that we were going to be talking about the oral microbiology manual I was writing.

When I arrived at the office the Dean, the Chair and the Program Coordinator for the programs I taught were there as well. I was very surprised as I thought I would be speaking with the program coordinator about the microbiology manual. Instead there was a red file folder in the middle of a circular table. They thanked me for coming down and said: "We are laying you off now - you could go home if you wish." I was in absolute shock. I could not believe this and I don't remember even asking why? I could not figure this out as I taught ten different courses during the academic year with about eight hundred students. I had a very heavy teaching load.

I managed to get upstairs into my office before I burst into tears. My self-esteem, my sense of self-worth and fulfillment had been totally wiped out with one statement. I understood grief and bereavement from a non-death perspective, being laid off was totally devastating to me.

I did go home that day and when I checked the mail the enrollment package for the Funeral Director course was in the mail.

I had not been listening. Perhaps God had been whispering in my ear and I did not take notice. With one statement, "we are laying you off, you can go home now if you like", the time was created to return to school for the fourth time and become a licensed Funeral Director. Another leap of faith.

I took this as a sign that I was to move on and enroll in the Funeral Service Education program. But before I did that I had to close the door on teaching at college. I set to work on gathering the information to appeal being laid off and set into motion the grievance process.

Reaching out to the Union Steward, I gathered as much information as I could, organized this information and filed a grievance. Unfortunately when colleagues hear that you are laid off, you become shunned and isolated and it becomes very challenging to find the specialized knowledge needed. The union was a fantastic resource. I organized this information and scheduled a hearing with the Vice President Academic. At this point, I had more education and more tenure than three other colleagues and had filed a grievance stating that they should be laid off and not myself. Working with the Union President we created a plan to move forward and prepare for this meeting.

Even though I challenged three colleagues' positions, as a person of faith and the serendipity of receiving the Funeral Service Education application in the mail the same day as I was laid off, I knew that I would not remain teaching at the college.

When I announced that I was dropping the grievance at this meeting, you have never seen so many grown people scuttle out of the room so fast. I had a private meeting with the Vice President Academic and was able to share my concerns with the administration in the Allied Health Sciences division.

In the fall of 1996 I enrolled in the Funeral Service Education program. At this point I was in my forties with three children and returning to school full time.

Was it academically, logistically, and financially challenging – absolutely! My leap of faith certainly took a lot of courage.

Yet anything is possible when you have a burning desire, make the decision in the spirit of faith, and formulate an organized practical plan to acquire specialized knowledge.

When I took the Funeral Services Education program there were three certifications: Funeral Director Class 1- Embalming; Funeral Director Class 2 – No Embalming; and Transfer Service Operator.

As a lifelong learner and a person who wants the full qualifications, I knew that I wanted the specialized knowledge of the Funeral Director Class 1.

The program was two years in length. The first year was the academic program at the college. The second year was an internship placement at a funeral home, with the practical requirement that you have to have embalmed at least fifty people.

During the academic year, I applied for and took the academic exemptions in Human Anatomy, Physiology, Pathology and Microbiology, as I had taught these courses at another college. Even with these exemptions, I found the course load very challenging. Yet I was persistent and determined that I would be successful in this program.

When the second year placements were coming up, my intention was to secure a placement at a funeral home close to my residence. My intention was realized, as I was extremely fortunate to work for a funeral home very close to home. The company owned two different locations at that time and I was able to work six months at each location. Even though it was the same owner the feel and clientele was very different at the two locations. I appreciated the opportunity to gather the specialized knowledge each had to offer.

At the successful completion of these requirements there is a practical examination to demonstrate that you can embalm a person, an academic exam and finally a legislation exam.

When I graduated in 1998 as a Class 1 Funeral Director I knew that I wanted to specialize in prepaid funeral planning, rather than work in a funeral home as a licensed funeral director. This decision allowed me the flexibility to be with my family in the evenings and on the weekends.

Prepaid funeral plans have always been available to people, yet in 1998 it was still relatively unknown. This definiteness of purpose very much fit into my organization and self-discipline as a teacher. I knew I could set my own appointments, be on time for the appointments and run my own schedule allowing for the needs of my young family.

I also imagined a new concept as to how prepaid funeral plans were available to people. I created the concept of a broker for prepaid funeral plans. I was able to secure alliances with different funeral homes in my geographical area and work independently to meet people, and help them set up the prepaid funeral plan that best fit their needs, and values. I am successful at this because I am self-motivated and I can control the conditions of how I work, allowing me to be financially successful and have a flexible schedule.

Very early on I realized that many people had an extremely vague notion of how to set up a prepaid funeral plan. Over and over my clients asked me, "don't you miss teaching?" My reply was and still is no, I am still teaching people daily about what has to be done and what can be done when setting up a prepaid funeral plan.

As the acceptance of prepaid funeral plans grew in the general population, and hundreds of thousands of dollars were placed into prepaid funeral accounts, the economic advantages available from prepaid funeral sales caught the attention of the insurance industry. This industry was lobbying to take control of the sales and mandate that people selling preneed funeral plans had to have their Life Insurance licenses. In 2000, I in enrolled in and completed the Level 1 and Level 2 licensing; for accident and sickness as well as life insurance and living benefits. Being a lifelong learner I was motivated to have this knowledge for myself and my clients. I was also planning ahead to take the Life Licenses before the requirements were increased significantly.

A few years later the Certified Senior Advisor (CSA) designation caught my attention. I phoned the organization to ask them about the course requirements. After a very informative conversation, I thanked them and reviewed the curriculum online. Later I contacted the owner of the program and asked to meet with her. We arranged a meeting the next week. I shared with her that I loved the program and also mentioned that the curriculum needed one more piece. The 'End of Life Planning" piece. That was another leap of faith.

I waited and she looked at me and said yes, you are absolutely right! I was so relieved; I took the CSA course and then wrote the End of Life Planning module for the curriculum. From that time in 2004, it has been a fantastic friendship and working relationship. This example reinforces for me that you never know until you try. Since this time the CSA designation has been redesigned and is now available as: the Age Friendly Business Consultant and the Certified Professional Consultant on Aging (CPCA).

In addition to the dearth of knowledge about the emotional and financial advantages of prepaid funeral plans; I noticed that my clients did not know how to set up an effective estate plan. I remember thinking there has to be a better way to educate people about this – how can I better serve my clients? Recognizing this gap and realizing that thoughts are things, I envisioned an adult baby book. There had to be a simple way to know what documents are important and why these documents are important. There had to be a simple way to organize these documents and let one's executor know what you have, why you have it, and what you want done with your assets when you die.

In the beginning I did not know how this would take shape. With the decision made to research and write this workbook, I started the organized planning. The outcome of my persistence and specialized knowledge is now available in digital or print format "Taking Care of Business" executor's workbook.

Acquiring specialized knowledge and training continues to be a strong motivator for me.

In 2014, I completed the Certified Executor Advisor (CICEA) designation. This is a fantastic course that helps me recognize where my clients can do thoughtful planning. The curriculum provides an overview of the duties and responsibilities of an Executor, and the Probate process and Administration of an Estate. What I especially found helpful were the sections on of how to administer the financial considerations, property, life insurances, and potential trusts in an Estate.

A more recent gap I noticed is that the role of being an executor is an arduous task for the average person. Banks and Trust companies offer assistance in this role yet this is generally only offered to high net worth clients. Not all people are high net worth clients. The rules, regulations and potential liability for an executor are enormous. Many of my clients are now calling on me to support them as their Certified Executor advisor. I am able to assist them in this capacity in two ways. First, I educate people and help them organize and streamline their Estate ahead of time, to make things easier for their Executor in the end. Or in the end, I support the Executor through the Estate reporting, evaluation, administration and closure process.

I am absolutely delighted that I am able to continue to educate people about what has to be done and what can be done to craft the absolute best estate plan and funeral arrangement to celebrate a loved one's life. The sense of relief and accomplishment my clients share with me is my motivation to continue educating and helping people out.

Reviewing my life to date through the lens of Napoleon Hill's "Think and Grow Rich" has reinforced my commitment to have the "courage to keep on keeping on" and continue to follow these cornersstones for my personal development and financial success. I look forward to taking yet another leap of faith.

BIO

KAT DOWNEY – M.Ed. CPCA CICEA

End of Life issues are never easy to talk about. However, the sooner we set up our final arrangements the better things will be for our family in the end. Kat Downey has a Master's degree in education, previously teaching at High School and Community College. As a licensed Funeral Director and Insurance Agent specializing in prepaid funeral plans, Kat has helped thousands of people set up their eventual funeral plans.

Kat's company, Legacy Matters, does an incredible job of helping people arrive at the absolute best Estate plan for their families. Throughout the process, they are able to save people a ton of time, money and potential chaos. They take what is often perceived as a complicated and dreary process and make it simple and effortless. Kat's clients feel ecstatic to get this process behind them. Their sense of accomplishment and peace of mind is evident when they are always commenting how much better they sleep at night knowing they have made the right decision that will positively impact their families forever.

Kat is widely recognized as an upbeat, honest and capable professional who leaves her clients feeling cared for and secure. She is a much sought after speaker and published author - specializing in Funeral and Estate preplanning. She spends a great deal of time doing group presentations using a fresh and lively approach to a once taboo subject.

For a complimentary Estate Evaluation you can connect with Kat at:

katdowney@legacymatters.ca   905-717-9197   www.legacymatters.ca

TO DREAM THE IMPOSSIBLE DREAM
By: Kathy Hadley

"Everything she has ever set her mind to accomplish she has."

That's what my Uncle told a very surprised banker once when he was co-signing a rather large loan for the expansion of one of my businesses.

It made me feel very proud.

Prior to this time, I had never realized that my Uncle had such a high opinion of my abilities to make things happen.

Being number five of nine children, from a moderate household, you would think I would just be resolved to the fact that I would never have anything I wanted in life.

But that is not the case at all.

Long before I ever read the book "Think and Grow Rich" by Napoleon Hill or any other self-help or empowerment book..

Long before I attended any seminars or motivational speeches…

Long before I ever hired a coach or mentor….

Long before any of my personal business successes….

There were the positive life examples of my grandmother and my mother.

These two women deeply affected me.

They both had a positive attitude about life. They always saw the glass as full. And they could find the good in almost every situation.

Let me share with you a little bit about my Grandmother so you can get a taste of her indomitable spirit.

My grandmother, although born in the United States, went with her father back to the country of Lebanon when she was only two years old.

It seemed like a crazy thing to do but at the time things were a challenge for my Grandmother's parents. Her mother was pregnant with their second child, they had businesses they were running, and her Grandmother was alone. After much discussion, they just decided to leave my Grandmother there. It was only meant to be for a short while. However, it didn't work out that way.

World War I broke out and my Grandmother was basically stuck there until she was 14 years old, being raised by her grandmother.

While in Lebanon, she had many happy times with her Grandmother living a simple life. Her Grandmother owned a small olive orchard. They worked the olive orchard and cooked and did household chores. The only schooling was what her Grandmother taught her at home.

My Grandmother told me many stories that increased my admiration for her strength. One such story was when there was an earthquake and the building she was in collapsed on her. The only thing that saved her from being crushed were 2 beams that had fallen against each other creating an inverted V over her. It took hours for the people of the village to dig her out and when they finally did, she was not breathing. They laid her on a table and the Priest began to give her Last Rights. In the middle of the sacrament, she let out a scream as if to come back to life and got up off of the table as if nothing had happened.

Another time, she was in the street and a runaway horse drawn wagon came right towards her. She was knocked down but somehow not only was she missed by the horse's hooves but by the wagon, too.

Both of these incidents were miraculous.

Her Grandmother was getting older and was afraid that if something happened to her, Flora, my Grandmother, would have no one to look after her. She sent a letter to her daughter and they arranged to have my Grandmother come back to the United States with a friend of the family.

The trip back to the United States took many months. My Grandmother was only 14 and was leaving the only home and the only Mother she ever knew. She did not remember anything other than that village. She knew no English, only Arabic. She did not even know her own parents or siblings. She had no idea what to expect.

During her long travels, all she had were the clothes on her back and a tiny bundle she tied up with a scarf that she could carry. Once they arrived at Ellis Island, they were held up there for 6 months because of an illness. Years later, there was a picture of the immigrants at Ellis Island and there was a little Lebanese girl with her little bundle and my Grandmother always thought it was her.

Finally being allowed to leave Ellis Island, they started the long journey across the United States to Southeast Kansas. Upon arriving home, it was not your normal loving family reunion. They did not even know each other. She literally was a stranger in her own family's home. The other siblings did not speak Arabic very well and my Grandmother spoke no English at the time.

It was a long first couple of weeks.

Things got much better when school started.

The entire family went to the Catholic Church and the children attended a make shift Catholic School in a little building in the alley behind where the current Church now stands. One of the Nuns took an immediate liking to my Grandmother and even though she knew no Arabic, they managed to communicate. In the course of just one school year, that wonderful Nun taught my Grandmother how to speak and read and write English and took her from kindergarten through the eighth grade in her studies.

Grandma's life started getting better and as the next several years went on, she met a man and they fell in love. He even bought her a diamond engagement ring. Well, the diamond was very tiny, but it was a diamond ring nonetheless.

But her hopes of marriage to her love were soon ended. She was informed by her parents that she had been promised to marry her second cousin. The parents of both had made these arrangements many years before as was the custom.

She did not know this cousin and only met him a few days before they were married.

Even with ALL of that, she always had a happy demeanor, she never complained, she kept a lovely, although modest, home, and raised her 3 children.

That is why she was such a wonderful role model for me.

She was always so positive and happy regardless of her circumstances and she made the best of everything without complaint.

In addition to my Grandmother, I had the encouragement of my mother, as well.

My mother was always so positive. If I ever wanted to try out for anything at school my mother always encouraged me. She would often say, "If you don't try, the answer is already 'no'. If you try, there is always a chance you may win."

Having that kind of inspiration to "try" whatever I wanted helped me go after many things in life.

One such thing I wanted was "the summer dress".

The Summer Dress story is one my mother and I both very much enjoy telling for different reasons.

My Mom likes to tell it from the perspective of how she was always listening to us even when we might think she was not.

And I like telling this story because it really illustrates how The Universal Laws and principles of Think and Grow Rich work even before you actually know them.

The Summer Dress story goes like this....

It was still mid-winter in our small town, yet all of the stores starting getting their spring and summer clothes in stock.

One of the higher priced boutiques down the street from our house had this summer dress in the window on display. I immediately fell in love with it. I decided right then and there I was going to have this dress.

Full of excitement for my new dress, I rushed home to tell my Mom all about it. When I got there, she was busy with one of the younger kids in the high chair and at the same time she was prepping some vegetables for dinner at the kitchen sink.

My excitement could hardly be contained as I described the dress in great detail. The cap sleeves, the fabric, the design of rows of thin lines with rows of tiny flowers between them, all angled like a V in the skirt and top. Halfway through my totally excited, effusive description, it looked to me as if my Mom was not really paying attention and my happiness turned to sadness.

As I turned to walk away thinking Mom wasn't listening, she stopped me. "Where are you going?" She asked.

"Oh, just to my room." I answered.

"But what about the dress?" she inquired, "When are you going to get it?"

I was surprised she heard a word I said about the dress and so turned around and told her just that.

"Mom", I didn't think you were listening…

"Of course, I was listening"… and she proceeded to describe the summer dress in great detail just as I had described it to her.

(That was about 40-years-ago and my Mom can still describe that dress.)

Back to the story - after describing the dress, she asked me, how much it cost.

Goodness!

I did not know.

I had not even gone inside to find out. I just saw the dress through the window and decided it was mine.

That night at dinner and that evening all I could think about was that dress. It was already mine even though I had no idea what it cost or how I would ever pay for it.

The next day, after school, I walked by the shop again and just stared through the window at it.

Finally, I just mustered up the courage to walk right in and find out about that dress. Remember, this was a high-end boutique but it did not matter to me. I was going to have that dress.

I tried it on and loved it even more than seeing it on the mannequin.

It was definitely for me.

I asked what the price was and it was so much money, I couldn't believe it but the price did not deter me from my decision that it was going to be mine.

With total confidence, I told the salesman all about how I had seen the dress in the window and how I had decided it was mine and told my mother all about it and on and on. Additionally, with total confidence, I asked him to hold it on lay-a-way for me and that I would make weekly payments on it.

I did not ask him if he had lay-away or if I could do this, I just asked about it, matter of factly. He wrapped it up in tissue paper and placed it nicely in a bag and he put my name on it. When he handed me the receipt, I was thrilled.

I immediately went home and excitedly told my mom what I had done and how I was going to pay for it.

The only thing is I had absolutely no idea HOW I would pay for it. I just knew I would pay for it.

After that I got really busy doing whatever I could to make money.

With the help of my mom, we put the word out that I could babysit, help with cleaning, and I even sold some of my belongings to the neighborhood kids.

Every week, I would go in and make whatever payment I could on this summer dress.

The winter turned to spring and the spring turned to summer and I kept working and making payments on my summer dress.

The summer was just about over when I finally made the last payment.

Once I got that dress home, I wanted to wear it all the time.

It was the biggest desire that I had fulfilled for myself up to that age in my life.

It was a HUGE accomplishment for me.

So much so, that I STILL have that summer dress hanging in my closet right now as an example of being able to create anything I want in my life with desire, visualization and willingness to work for it.

By the way, I was only 13 at the time. That store closed just a few years later. Many years later, by happenstance, I met up with that storeowner and I found out that they never did have a "lay away" plan. He just did that for me because of my excitement and determination.

Since then, there have been many things that I decided to do and achieved them with absolutely no idea ahead of time how I was going to do it.

I just knew I was going to do it.

That is what I mean by "Dream the Impossible Dream". Most of the things or situations I wanted and ended up creating in my life I had absolutely no idea HOW I was going to do it. I just decided that I was going to do it.

Then, I started reading self-help and empowerment books and read "Think and Grow Rich.

It was in reading Napoleon Hill's precepts that I realized that this is how I had lived my life up to now.

He starts off the book talking about a 'Secret' and that some people will discover what this 'secret" is and others may not.

It is that 'Secret' that has shaped my life, and now, I help others learn these precepts and apply them to their lives for success and happiness.

When Napoleon Hill wrote Think and Grow Rich in 1937 he probably expected the book to be a success and he expected to change the lives of many people, but he probably did not expect the continued success of the book so many years later or that his book would change the entire personal success genre.

From the book's initial publication in 1937 until Napoleon Hill's death in 1970, Think and Grow Rich sold over 20 million copies.

Since then sales have multiplied many times over.

The book frequently hits best-seller lists, even in the 21st century.

More importantly, however: the teachings have multiplied.

Napoleon Hill's philosophy can now be found re-stated and repackaged in many books, e-books, audio, video, and blogs, by the numerous authors who have taken Hill's basic philosophy, expanded on it or scaled it down, reworded it and made it their own.

It is not surprising, almost 80 years after its first publication; Hill's lessons are as timely as ever.

In Think and Grow Rich he has divided the lessons into 13 principles to be mastered: Desire, Faith, Auto-suggestion, Specialized knowledge, Imagination, Organized planning, Decision, Persistence, the Power of the master mind, the Mystery of sex transmutation, the Subconscious mind, the Brain, and the Sixth sense.

Desire

Of all of the principles in Think and Grow Rich, the principle of Desire is no doubt the most important of all.

For this reason, Hill placed it at the very beginning of his book.

To understand what Hill means by Desire, it is important to forget all ideas of just daydreaming or wishful thinking that the word may hold. Hill's Desire is not about wishing, as wishes may or may not come true, and usually require the action of some outside person or thing to make them happen.

No. What he is talking about is Intention.

Making a decision that just will be no matter what.

Just like the decision I made when I saw the summer dress.

Only when a person truly decides with intention something that is wanted do they take wholehearted and what I call "inspired" action towards attaining, that which is wanted.

Where wishing is more often just hoping, "deciding what you want" is well defined and commits to a course of action.

When the desire and intention for something is fully developed, and it is working for you subconsciously at all hours of the day, you have got it!

To ensure that your wants become Desire, Hill proposes taking some time to develop a clear and concise statement of that Desire. It is important, he argues, to be very specific.

I would add to be as specific as it feels good to you and no more.

If the Desire is to have money, the amount of money can be specified or the lifestyle that represents that certain amount of money can be visualized.

If it is too general, the Desire turns into a wish or something to just hope for.

Hill also felt that it is important to establish when the goal is to be achieved and what service or good will be exchanged in turn for the achieving of the goal.

This should all come together in an action plan, which will be revisited often to imprint the Desire in the mind.

The reader who has read enough self-help books will recognize this advice.

The importance of having a clear goal, for one's happiness and for the achieving of that goal, is undisputed today.

And just like my "summer dress" and everything else I have created in my life, it is so much more than just a wish.

It is a definite decision, an intention with total clarity and certainty.

From that decision, a plan of action is created and the decision and the plan of action will engulf you. It will become part of your being.

When this happens, your desire will manifest.

As I have demonstrated here, these principles work with other things besides money…. like my summer dress.

But let me elaborate on the story I started this chapter with of my Uncle helping me with the business loan from the bank…

For that, let me go back a bit to how I got to the point of needing a business loan in the first place.

Every big thing I had wanted to accomplish in my life up to this point, I had done, never knowing HOW I was going to do it.

I got to college, I got my accounting degree, I moved away from home, I got the job I wanted at that point, I passed the CPA exam and now I was ready to open a business.

(Each one of those items I manifested have their own story but those will be saved for a future book.)

I had gotten an idea for a business and just like my "summer dress", I was obsessed with thinking about it.

My mind was on my new business so much that I could not really keep my attention on my accounting work anymore.

It was time for me to give my one-month notice, help them find my replacement and put all of my attention on my new business idea.

While I was finishing up my last month at my job, I started looking for locations, creating a logo, getting brochures and everything else needed for my new business.

Being an accountant, I got all of the figures together and budgeted it all out so that I would NOT have to borrow any money to open.

And being very enthusiastic and determined to make this successful, I just knew that I would start making money right away.

Actually, I had to. I was spending my entire life savings including my retirement fund to make this happen and I was single at the time. As soon as my job was over, I would have no other source of income. I gave myself no safety net. I was intent on this all going well.

We were ready to open and I had been training employees for the 2 weeks before the scheduled open day when a really huge (well, huge for me at the time) setback and expense occurred.

The location I was leasing had not updated the bathroom to comply with the American's with Disability Act (ADA). The toilet was 1 inch too close to the wall. This bathroom had nothing to do with the renovations I had made to the location. I had not done anything in the bathroom. But since we had made other updates, we had to get an inspection and the bathroom did not pass.

Long story short, I had to have the concrete floor jack hammered up and the plumbing moved one inch and then replaced to meet the ADA standards.

This added 2 weeks to my timeline on opening and an unexpected $6000 cost to my total budget.

However, that was not all...

Remember I said I had already hired my employees---I could not just let them go.

So I also had the additional cost of the employees for the added 2 weeks WITHOUT any funds coming in yet.

You would think that the added costs of plumbing and delays and employees would have been enough to make me need to get a loan.

But that was not it at all.

When I first started all of this, I knew that things generally go over time and over budget no matter how much you plan so I had a contingency.

But now, my contingency plan was even running thin.

(A side note about all of this, I learned a lot about negotiating leases and what to make sure the landlord pays for in all my future locations.)

So here we are, ready to open for businesses.

I had started my advertising early and then there was that plumbing setback but still I was determined to do well.

There I was, in my new business with my new employees on opening day and there was nobody coming in.

Standing there looking out the front glass door, knowing I had to make a go of this, I took a bunch of brochures and started handing them out to all the surrounding businesses and residences.

Within a few hours, we had clients coming in....

And it never let up.

It was a complete success.

So why did I need the loan then?

This is the funny part.

After all of that, I did not need a loan to stay in business because of increased costs.

I had so many happy clients that they told others about the business and people contacted me to open a location of their own. I had only planned for one location. I had not planned to become a franchise.

It was actually the fast expansion and success of the one location that caused me to ask my Uncle to co-sign a 90 day $50,000 note for me to get through the expansion hump while sales continued to increase.

And that is how I ended up sitting with my Uncle and a banker hearing my Uncle say in response to the banker asking, "Why would you risk $50,000 to help your niece?"

And my Uncle said, "Everything she has ever set her mind to accomplish she has."

You can, too!

I hope that these stories have encouraged you to take the first steps to everything you want in life.

THINK and grow anything you want.

Kathy Hadley

Bio:

Kathy Hadley, known as the "life coach to life coaches" around the world, believes her mission is to help people live the life they truly want. With her long 25-year reputation and her more recent experience with a worldwide networking group, she is a top advisor and expert to help life coaches and clients achieve their maximum peak potential.

"What I stress the most is that we all have the potential to tap into our unlimited possibility within" says Hadley. "My goal is to de-mystify Universal Laws and give people real, measurable, tangible results."

Her approach is direct, straightforward and to-the-point. Her matter of fact approach is what draws men and women from all over the world to her website, products and classes online. http://kathyhadleylifecoach.com

In 2014, Hadley launched new updates on her Facebook page https://www.facebook.com/kathyhadleylifecoach that is designed to reach the audience of men and women who are ready for change in their life. She aims to attract the 21-65 crowd and help them use Universal Laws and practical principles like from the book "Think and Grow Rich" by Napoleon Hill to increase their wealth, increase their health, and increase their happiness in life.

MY JOURNEY TO THINK AND GROW RICH
By: Karren E. Henderson

Vision: See Yourself There

MY Journey to Think and Grow Rich

Connecting the Dots

When I was growing up I cannot recall peer pressure to the extent it made me feel bad or less than my peers. We grew up different, period. In our household, our religious beliefs were different, our daily practices were different, we observed the Sabbath, we did not eat pork or shellfish and all of this was very normal for us and we liked it and even loved it. We did not observe traditional holidays. Christmas was just another day along with New Year's Eve. I can remember a couple of my classmates who received leather coats for Christmas one year and it was a big deal. When Patricia and Diane received their leather coats that Christmas, I felt a tinge of "wow, wish I had one". It was not a feeling of I wanted to have one so badly that I was jealous, upset, and threw a temper tantrum (by the way, you did not throw temper tantrums in my home). First of all, I rationalized that both girls being only children, it was easier for their parents to buy a leather coat for them. There were six children in my family and one parent on a daily basis, because my father was in the military and my mother did not travel with him.

We were raised with a very pragmatic philosophy by a woman who believed in her religion and discipline and lived for her children. Raising six children as a single parent was not easy, even for a very devoted and dedicated parent. "Go to school and get a good education and get a job. If you want to go to college, you will have to work, go at night and pay for it yourself!" This was a daily mantra because my mother saw her children working to sustain themselves first and hopefully not experiencing the same financial challenges she had raising us. School was very important in our household and we were held to high expectations.

See Yourself There

My mother would always tell the story of how my father had purchased the house we grew up in for the family and they had moved there from an apartment. So the house was very large to my mother at the time and she was pregnant with me, her fourth child and my father was leaving for a tour of duty overseas and for her entire pregnancy she was always scared. Scared because she was without her husband, in a big new house with three young children and pregnant. As a result of these conditions, my mother said all of her fear during the pregnancy fell on me. I was scared of everything; fire engine sirens, animals, doctor's offices, needles, blind people. I was deathly afraid of blind people. As a small child, I always thought they were coming after me, so much so that once let go of my mother's hand in the street, ran away, and was hit by a car. It was not until I became an adult that I was able to assist a blind person across the street without feeling a tinge of discomfort and fear.

As the fourth child, I had a brother seven years older than me, a sister two years older, and another brother one year older than me! I remembered very clearly how I always wanted to keep up with my older siblings. I wanted to read their books, play their games, and be with their friends which I found to be much more desirable than just being with my friends. Consequently, I was always slightly ahead in my classes, which was really fun. I loved school and was the teacher's helper, and they were always giving me something extra, like a book to read, an assignment for extra credit. It may not have been a book that the class was reading, but a different book that kept me slightly ahead of the class. I loved to read and I felt so special when my teacher gave me an extra book to read!!

Using Your Mind

I attended a vocational high school, which prepared me with a skill that enabled me to get a job right after high school. Business Education was my course of study because I intended to get a job downtown in one of the office buildings.

This program was very attractive to me because I was focused on getting a job more than anything and "having my own" stuff!! Money to get my own place and get a car and buy clothes and simply be independent was the epitome of being an adult (in my mind at that time). I wanted to go to college but having to pay for it seemed like something I would have to do by taking classes at night and that made getting my degree seem so far away. I always wanted to be successful and I realized much later and did achieve some semblance of success, but my dreams were not big enough. Upon reflection, and this is true for others as well, if the teacher appeared, I was not ready. I was on the fringe of having the car that I did not know how to drive. What could have helped in that time is to know that I needed to write down my goals, yes something as simple as that I did not do. My drive to succeed by getting employment after high school resulted in getting a job in an office building downtown, but as a file clerk. While it was great getting a job, I met an older woman after a day or two and she shared with me that she had been working there for 20 years and I asked innocently, "as a file clerk" and she proudly responded "yes"!!! In that moment, I knew I had accepted the wrong job and had to get out of there fast.

By the way, this job was located on Madison Ave and I felt some sense that I had arrived but it did not go with the picture in my mind. I was very young and I thought since Madison Avenue was the advertising capital that to work on Madison Avenue was something extraordinary. Obviously, I had so much to learn, but I knew I could not stay in this firm where someone spoke proudly of being in the same position for 20 years. I knew I could not grow here so I had to make a change immediately. On day three at my new job I had gotten an interview on my lunch hour for a keypunch operator position. The keypunch test that was administered lasted so long that I knew I would not be able to return to my very new place of employment. Additionally, I still did not know if I had passed the keypunch test and the thought of not having any job at the end of the day was too much to even contemplate. I ended up getting the keypunch position and later learned I had done so well on the test, that they just let me keypunching!

What I realized without it being pointed out to me is that I wanted to achieve and be successful without achievement and success being clearly defined at that time. At this particular point in my life (in the early 70's), having a position with a reputable firm with the ability to grow and be promoted was an absolute success. I often think about my tenure at CBS in the News Division. I was a keypunch operator for the CBS/NYT surveys, a position that I got as a temporary assignment. Everyone was so nice and tables of food were provided for the entire staff. I was so impressed. I can remember letting the person in charge know I would be pleased if they requested me from my temporary agency whenever they needed a keypunch operator. That assignment resulted in a full-time position with CBS. A new department was created and there was a position for one keypunch operator, I was hired and one computer operator, and we became the computer department in the Election Unit of the CBS News Division.

I can remember after two or three years as a keypunch operator, I approached my manager and informed her that I was tired of working with my hands and wanted to use my head. Yes, I know, not very sophisticated or professional, but apparently my manager had the same thought in mind in terms of me moving up the ladder. She shared with me that she had a position in mind for me that she believed I was ready to handle as Supervisor of Data Processing. I was so shocked and pleased with the ease in which this transition was taking place. It was a happy day for me, but there was still another shock to come and that was my replacement as a keypunch operator. I was replaced with three new keypunch operators. Needless to say, I was stunned because I never thought it would take three people to do the same amount of work that I did and I was never offered three salaries. Of course, education comes in many forms and the least of which may be the classroom!

My Purpose and Special Gift

When I think about it now, it is ironic to me how I never thought in terms of my purpose or thought about any special gifts I possessed. I did not give any particular attention to it at all. I was always positive, loyal, and a hard worker because those qualities were instilled in all of us in our home.

I think of the many compliments people have given to me over the years, my drive, how motivating I am, always willing to help someone or help in some situation. When people guess my profession they think I am either a teacher or lawyer. It does not matter how long I may have known the person, it could even happen in a cab ride and the subject comes up in conversation, it is usually the same guess that is made. It all comes back to me helping people to see the bright side of a situation (or the silver lining as the common phrase goes), and the hope that always exist as long as there is life!!

I realize now and accept as my definite purpose is to inspire and motivate, women in particular, with the specific intent to empower them to see their worth, influence their belief system and relaunch their lives by recapturing unfulfilled dreams and making new ones. BELIEF! VISION! FAITH! To understand that to dream, and put plans in place to realize those dreams is a necessary action to take. WHY? The mere thought of knowing that you can make your dreams as big or bigger than you ever imagined; to change your life for a specific purpose and commit to work hard until you achieve and realize your dreams is truly motivating. WHY? To change the mindset of future generations so that it becomes the norm to pursue greatness! It is also important that I inspire, influence, guide, and motivate the youth in my family to understand how money works, go to college without getting a student loan and understand the mission in college is to get a good education, study the behavior of college students, for the expressed purpose of learning what kind of people you would like to hire, versus those you would not like to hire. Always operate from the standpoint that you are building your own business. Jobs are what you will offer others but you will have your own business. What would this world look like if the entrepreneurial concept was the norm?

THINK AND GROW RICH

The writings of Napoleon Hill have definitely impacted my pursuit of wealth and prosperity, as well as helped me focus on my definite purpose. I no longer have the stigma of believing that wealth is not something I should be pursuing. I understand now that it was a mindset that was crafted and instilled in me for most of my life that prevented me from realizing that I did not dream big enough! I could do anything I set my mind to do. Certainly, I understood being focused and setting my mind to a task or goal, but what has really been the revelation for me is how low I set the bar. So many instances in my own life when I put out into the universe what I wanted to achieve, I got just that and no more. We all too often think we do not deserve more so we do not get more. "A mind is a terrible thing to waste"! How many times have you heard and or uttered this phrase? Did you or do you really understand and appreciate the meaning and significance of this statement?

One very important experience that I appreciated in school was the emphasis placed on teamwork and team dynamics. I vowed to learn to work to the best of my ability with whatever team I was assigned because out in the world you do not know who you are going to work with or have to interact with and to have some insight into a diverse group of people and how to get along so that you achieve whatever your goal might be is an asset.

Although I thought I really missed out on something vital in my life when I did not attend college right after high school, the value and immediate application of what I learned later in life far exceeds, I believe, the value that I might have obtained at that time. This thought continued a long time and made me feel "less than" – One day while working at CBS in the news division, I shared my insecurities with one of our statisticians, and he said to me, "Who do the top managers come to around here?" Who do they consult with?" The answer to those questions was "ME" and while it gave me a new perspective and self-awareness, doubt and insecurity still lingered, but I held on to that new perspective.

A year ago I was introduced to a business opportunity at a time when my entrepreneur IQ was rising and I wanted to do more than I was doing to generate additional income. This opportunity also opened my eyes to the tax benefits that I would be entitled to just by having a home-based business. This was extremely interesting to me because I needed some tax deductions and I also wanted to employ my son who had been unemployed for a couple of years. What I had no way of knowing and therefore did not anticipate was the self-development I would receive just being a part of this endeavor. I have entered a place where I belong, with a business that enables me to help people, build a legacy for my family and all of that is wonderful. But it touches me in the heart and soul of who I truly am – A Giver, A Helper, One Who Inspires Others, A Child of God, A Motivator, A Teacher and I can take me and build empires because I have tapped into the Greatness in me and I am on my journey happily pursuing my definite purpose in life. Some years ago, I had this book Think and Grow Rich but very little of it do I recall from years ago. Reading it now, however, enhances my Belief, and allows me the Vision to See Myself while Using My Mind and Connecting the Dots. Growth and growing, this life is a continuing education and I am grateful for all of the teachers that I have had and the lessons I have learned from all they have taught me and the opportunity I now have to rework, revise, and relearn the lessons to achieve my true Greatness. I am honored and grateful to have arrived at this time and place in my life.

BIO

Karren E. Henderson is Chief of Staff at Linneman Associates, and Senior Manager with MWR Life. She always believed in personal and professional development and achieved management level positions prior to completing her undergraduate degree in 2006. Previously, she was a Business Administrator at the Wharton School of the University of Pennsylvania and Supervisor of Data Processing at CBS, Inc. in the News Division.

Ms. Henderson has served on the Advisory Board of Dobbins Vocational High School and as a board member of the New Freedom Theatre. Her passion is to inspire and motivate the youth in her family to dream BIG, get a great education, learn how money works, and become entrepreneurs.

Ms. Henderson is the mother of three sons, eight grandchildren, and three great grandchildren. She currently resides in Philadelphia, PA, and has lived and worked in New York, NY, and Chicago, IL. An avid reader, tennis enthusiast, she loves to travel and go to the theatre.

Ms. Henderson has been in an administrative position for most of her career, starting as a keypunch operator, to a business administrator, event planner, executive assistant to the CEO. An Entrepreneur, former President of the Parents Group of Freedom Theater, Past board member of Freedom Theater, formerly on the Advisory Board of Business Education at Dobbins Vocational High School, former Co-Chair of the Employee Concerns Committee at University of Pennsylvania. A mother of three sons, a grandmother, and a great-grandmother building a legacy for her family.

Karren E. Henderson can be reached at:

Karren_h_2000@yahoo.com - 215 820 5158

www.MakeWealthReal.com/1120

FROM ZERO TO HERO
By: Jessica Higdon

"Thoughts mixed with definiteness of purpose, persistence, and a burning desire are powerful things."
-Napoleon Hill

I will never forget the first day I read Think and Grow Rich by Napoleon Hill. I was in an airplane on my way to visit my family in Cleveland, Ohio and I could not put it down. Every sentence made me question who I was as a person and the life I had started to create for myself. After reading the book I changed my thinking, my vision and no question my entire life for the better. I am forever grateful.

Before becoming a fervent student of personal development and entrepreneurship, I was totally insecure and had NO clue that I would eventually own my own successful business.

Business to me meant hard work with little payoff. To be frank, I had always wanted to own my own business but never wanted to do the work to get there. I was ambitiously lazy. I wanted all of the perks but could not get out of my own way to make it happen. As I was finishing up college I pretty much gave up on the dream I had to be an entrepreneur and wanted to do the "practical" thing, which was to get a job.

When I was 21 years old, I started working at a makeup counter to pay my bills. I hated going into that makeup counter every day. Do not get me wrong, I loved makeup but I hated the people I worked with. They all seemed so depressed and frustrated with life. To me, this was a great job with good benefits, but I was young. To most of the women, this was where they "settled" and many of them had been there for 20 plus years because they felt this was the best they could do.

In my opinion, everything happens for a reason…

I started comparing myself to the women that absolutely hated their jobs and their lives. The job was great, and by most people's standards we made decent money but most of them could not make themselves happy because they knew they were meant for more.

I could see the resentment oozing through their pores every day on the job, and I could not help but think, This could be me!" I thought to myself "What if I know I am meant for more, but I do not take the risk and try because I am afraid of a little 'work??' That's just silly."

I had been holding myself back from what I was capable of because I was afraid of responsibility. I thought I was too young and too shy to be a business owner. I thought I would hate working all of the time and that 'life is meant to be enjoyed, not endured.'

What I did not realize was that you can actually have it all! You CAN have a thriving business, and absolutely LOVE the work that goes with it. You CAN be young, a woman, and be a millionaire. You CAN absolutely improve your social skills with some personal development.

At the time I did not realize these things but knew I needed a big time mind shift. That's when I started voraciously searching for a mentor. I found one and decided to embrace an area I knew I could be whoever I wanted to be and no one would judge me, social media.

After 6 months of absolutely no income trying to work with the network I had close to me, I knew I needed to change things up and thought social media would be a great new avenue. At first I was scared and unsure that I was doing the right things but I trusted in those that had success before me and learned to just trust the process.

I changed my social media profiles around, and started reaching out to people on social media about my business and did so extremely consistently.

Every day without fail I would contact 20 plus people about my product. Results were a bit slow at first, but after 30 days I started to have some traction and made my first sale. From there I had all the confidence in the world that I was on the right track. Long story short, after 18 months of consistent action and lots of ups and downs, I had my first $10,000 month and went on to create a thriving 6 figure business.

Everyone kept asking me how I did it and they wanted me to teach my social media system to them. To serve the home business profession as a whole, my husband and I opened a training company that coaches business owners and entrepreneurs all over the world. I still pinch myself that that company now does multiple 7 figures a year, and to think I started out as a scared 21-year-old frantically searching for a strategy to make her first sale. It is amazing with time, passion, and hard work what you can accomplish.

"Assemble an Attractive Personality"
-Napoleon Hill Principle.

Had I not understood this, I mean REALLY understood it, my business today would not exist. I thought I had a decent personality and that it was honestly something that could not be changed. Sometimes we have beliefs that we are who we are and that "people don't change" (Have you ever heard that one?). That is SO far from the truth it is ridiculous.

I knew that, in order to be a leader, I had to act like a leader did. Whenever you want what someone has, the simplest way to get it is to do what he or she did and also act how they act. That does not mean you don't throw in your own personality and flare, but for instance, if your mentor is confident, then YOU must also portray confidence. If your mentor is complimentary, YOU must also be complimentary. Maybe not in the exact way that they are, but there is a reason they got to where they are and you are not there yet.

I started out shy and afraid. I knew the quickest way to the top was being confident but not cocky, outgoing but not obnoxious and giving but not sappy. I took all of those personality traits into consideration when approaching people about my business.

What I absolutely LOVE about social media, is that you can start over. Most people on there do not know you. They do not know that you do not have any business experience or were a dork in high school. All they know is what they see and what you allow them to see. That does NOT mean you should lie to your audience. Quite the contrary. It means you can become the person you were always meant to be. You can become the REAL you without feeling judged or weird about it.

Napoleon Hill taught me how to overcome my fears and shift into the person I need to be without worrying about what others will think. Remember the pleasing personality principle in whatever business you are in.

Business on Social Media – Is it worth it?

As women, I think we are inherently good at social media. We have a knack for great pictures and inspiration, however, where I see a lot of women lacking is actually MAKING MONEY from their social media. Facebook, Twitter, Instagram, and social media in general, are a ton of fun, but how do you actually monetize these sites without it becoming a full-time job?

I am a big believer in networking. Not just because a home business foundation is just that, a network; but because I believe you need networking in ANY business you are going to be a part of.

Think about it…

Do this exercise with me really quickly. Close your eyes, and imagine your dream business…

What platform is your business on? Online? Brick and Mortar?

How will you make your product or deliver your service?

Who will buy from you?

Who will fulfill the product/service for you?

Ok now open your eyes. Ask yourself this final question...

What part, if any, of that vision DOES NOT involve people? Business is run by people from start to finish. There may be automation in between, but NOTHING gets done without people. We are all in the people business at the end of the day, and that is what makes social media so important.

There are billions of new people to tap into on social media that are searching for a solution to their problems and you may just have that solution with your product or service. Without social media you greatly reduce your customer base. The foundation of social media, just like anything else, is people and if you understand how they think, what they want and how to get it to them, you have just become a master businesswoman.

Where do I start on Social Media?

A common question I get asked from our clients is "where do I start?" The internet and especially social media can get overwhelming and exhausting. Remember that everyone has to start somewhere and you can only eat an elephant one bite at a time.

Remember, that there is no substitute for good old-fashioned prospecting and reaching out to potential clients. Many people want to start with marketing, advertising and "comfortable" ways of generating leads. The problem is that marketing takes some time to get up and running and without a huge following already in place, you are going to have to go out there, get uncomfortable and hunt for the sale.

A typical daily routine for someone with a new business or a business that has not been generating a lot of sales may look like this:

-Add 10 new friends/fans

-Send first message/chat to start a conversation

-One piece of content – (blog, video, facebook live video, etc.)

-Share a piece of inspiration

-Follow up with new contacts and see if they are open to your business It is really as simple as that.

As human beings and especially women, we try to overcomplicate everything. If something seems to simple or too easy we will usually find a reason why it will not work. For some reason we are wired to do that. It's crazy isn't it?

DO NOT overcomplicate these steps. By just showing up for your business every day, you are doing more than 99% of the population.

One of Napoleon Hill's 17 Principles of Success is Self-Discipline. This is how I see that principle and this is a simple daily mantra to follow:

1. Show up every day

2. Show up with Excellence

3. Show up with the intention "To Serve"

Number three is where I see people struggle greatly, especially if you need money NOW. It is all too common for business owners to start prospecting and hunting for the sale ONLY with the intention of making money. First of all, if you go in with the expectation that everyone is going to make you money, you will only set yourself up for disappointment. Second, your potential customer or client can feel that energy and will never buy from you. If you approach people with the sole intention of finding out if they have a problem you can solve, or if they even have a need for your product or service, you will come out with a completely different and much better result. When you reach out to people on social media do so with the intention of making a friend and finding out if they have a problem you can solve. By just understanding that concept you will be ahead of 90% of the entrepreneurs out there.

Road Blocks Along the Way

I would not feel right about sharing my story if I did not tell you about the struggles I have encountered along the way. My hope is that you will learn from my mistakes, and if you happen to make them yourself, or run into any road blocks, you will understand that it is just par for the course and a totally normal experience.

I am far from perfect and being an entrepreneur reminds me of this OFTEN. There is literally no situation where you or I will always succeed. Failure, as I am sure you have heard, is not an option. How we choose to deal with failure, however, is!

The first year of my business was by far the most difficult. I would stick to my daily routine day in and day out and I was getting little to no traction. I made some sales, so I knew it worked, but I wanted more momentum. If I kept doing what I was doing forever it would have literally exhausted me in every regard.

Finally, after a LOT of hard work and frustration, I recruited a team member into my business that was a true leader. He had a large network and could easily bring me a ton of business. I was excited and felt like all of my hard work had FINALLY paid off! I made a ton of money in 24 hours, more than I had made for an entire 6 months! "It works!" I thought to myself. "Owning your own business, entrepreneurship, home businesses they actually work!" I was honestly so elated that I cried from joy. Then I got a terrible phone call....

This "leader" was in Singapore, so I had not actually had much contact with him. People in my business worked with people in Asia all of the time, so I did not think much of it, all I saw were the numbers. We chatted a few times and I thought "this is my big break!" When I spoke to my business partner I was told me that the numbers and accounts were all fake, and that all the money I had just earned was a complete scam! My heart sank. I questioned my business, my sanity, everything. Was what I was doing just a complete farce? Do people ACTUALLY succeed? Are all of those success stories of people being homeless to making millions actually true or is it all a complete lie?!

Those were the questions running through my head. My thoughts went from positivity to instant negativity for the entire day. I literally climbed into a corner of my house, curled up into a ball and started balling my eyes out. The frustration I felt in that moment was so intense that I felt like punching a hole in the wall and screaming at the top of my lungs. I had visions of breaking everything in my house! If you have ever felt this way, you know how intense adrenaline mixed with frustration can be.

I was angry, frustrated beyond belief and depressed in that moment. I picked up Think and Grow Rich to pull me out of my funk. At first I hated every word on the page. I felt like it was directly patronizing me every chance it could, as if the book was against me, which was just ridiculous. I knew I was just getting in my own way so I took a deep breath, closed my eyes for a minute and just released all of my emotions. I then went back into the book and it really started to sink in that this was a test.

Often, before our biggest breakthroughs, we have our biggest breakdowns. I was having a breakdown, so I thought I must be on the verge of a major breakthrough.

The next day, I went back to business as usual. I was still a little down but felt much better. Then I went back at it the next day, and the next day, and the next day, and nothing happened. I tried to keep my emotions separate from the result, and instead just be addicted to the activity. I knew, because others had done it, that if I just stayed with the activity the odds were in my favor. I could not help but succeed.

Long story short, the fifth day after my breakdown I received my biggest leader into the business and they created a ton of sales. He produced $245,000 in sales in 45 days. That was my big breakthrough. I had my first $10,000 earnings month and from there it got easier and easier to scale.

Whenever you feel like you want to quit, and you will, or you are questioning everything you are doing, and you will, or you feel like you just cannot do one more sales call, remember that before every major breakthrough there is usually a breakdown. It is almost as if the universe is testing you to see if you are worthy of the next level. This has been true my entire life. The breakdowns do not get easier, and they can even become more stressful, but you learn how to handle them and the breakthroughs are ten times more powerful!

Last Minute Thoughts

I hope my story has inspired you to veraciously go after your business with excitement. You are a different kind of woman just for reading this book, and you should embrace your drive and talents and never let anyone tell you anything is impossible.

BIO:

Jessica Higdon started in the network marketing industry when she was 21 years old. Because of her age and lack of business connections she had a very very small warm market. After striking out with friends and family and not signing up anyone in her business for the first 5 months, she decided to turn to Social Media.

Over the next 18 months, Jessica built a 6 figure residual income in her company using mainly Facebook & became the #1 female income earner. Her and her husband now train for the profession all over the world, and she has since created multiple training programs that have grossed over a million dollars in revenue. She has a serious passion for helping people grow their business from wherever they are currently.

BREAKING THE CYCLE
By: Sandra C. Pascal

I have asked myself a million times, "What does it take for a parent to want to kill their own child?" When I was 16 years old my father woke me up at gunpoint. That has been one of the worst days of my life and one of the biggest blessings. I know that sounds crazy. Trust me, I know. I spent many years high, drunk and lost because of that night. I remember waking up and seeing the gun in my face and feeling a sense of disbelief. My mother rushed into my room and pulled him away. Unfortunately, he turned on her and beat her. He dragged her out the of the house and beat her over and over and over again. I gathered my siblings as my heart pounded so hard that I felt that I was about to have a heart attack.

I hid my little brother and sister under my bed and ran to the china cabinet, pulled out a gun, walked outside and pointed it at him. I could hear my heart beat so loudly that it felt like it was in surround sound. I tried my best to hold the gun and keep my eye on the target. It is surreal to think about that moment. I was faced with the decision of killing my father in order to save my mother.

It all seemed to be happening in slow motion. Until my 6-year old brother's cries for help interrupted my train of thought. My next memory is of the police dragging my father away and seeing my mother on the sidewalk bleeding, crying and gasping for air. As I stood outside holding my siblings and wiping away their tears I knew that things would never be the same.

My mother was badly beaten but she was alive. I watched the sunrise with my siblings and wondered what would happen next. I had hoped that this would be the end of my father living with us. Maybe now we could move on and put his abuse and alcoholism behind us. Maybe this was a blessing and finally my mother would leave him. Maybe this was a new beginning for us. Maybe the living nightmare was finally over. It actually had just escalated to a whole new level of crazy. A few days later he returned to our home and the nightmare continued. I knew at that very instant that I needed to plan an exit strategy. It was clear that I no longer was a 16-year-old teenager, going to school, working on projects, hanging out with friends, or going to the mall. I was a 16 year who needed to plan a way to get out of my home. All of this happened in Colombia, South America. We had been living there for a year.

I was born and raised in Tenafly, NJ. We moved to Colombia when I was 15. My father had left us when I was 13 and my mom thought that moving to Colombia was the right thing to do. God only knows how hard I tried not to move there. I knew that something terrible would happen if we moved there to be with him. Since I was 15 I had no say in the matter. I tried talking to school counselors and one of my friends tried having his parents adopt me. It was a desperate time in my life. I had plans to go to Harvard and being a superstar soccer player. Instead I was put on a plane and forced to live with a sociopath.

Tenafly, NJ is one of the most incredible and magical places on earth. I can imagine people reading this and thinking. Tenafly? Magical? To me it was and always will be. It was not easy growing up there. It is a very affluent city. My classmate's parents were high-powered attorneys, celebrities, doctors, and stockbrokers and I was the daughter of a factory worker and housekeeper whose monthly combined income was equal to my friend's monthly allowance.

Our house was the size of most of my friend's garages and I got my clothes from the Salvation Army donation bin. We did not even go and buy our clothes at the Salvation Army, we would drive up to the donation bins late at night and grab the big black trash bags filled with clothes and take them back home. I used to be so embarrassed and would pray that no one would ever see us. The older I got the harder it was to fit in and feel equal. I was very blessed to have some of the most incredible teachers in the whole world. I will forever be grateful to all those men and woman who provided me with a safe haven 8 hours a day.

While most kids hated going to school, I loved it. School to me was a safe, loving and special place. At least for 8 hours a day I could be at peace and not surrounded by yelling and screaming, disrespect and betrayal. My town is magical because if I had never been exposed to that kind of wealth, abundance and incredible education I would not be where I am today. I remember as I far back as 3rd grade dreaming that one day I would be a successful and powerful woman. I would live a life full of abundance. That little girl has now lived her dreams and continues to dream even bigger. I wish I could say that that was it and that I lived happily ever after. I do live a wonderful life now however, there were many more obstacles and hardships to come after that night.

At 18 I was able to buy a one-way ticket back to New Jersey and start my life. I got on that plane and never looked back. One suitcase and a heart full of guilt because I was leaving my siblings behind in the house of horrors. Within a few months of being back in the United States I was offered a job at a bank and for once in my life I felt that things were on the right track. I also fell in love for the first time and began my life as a young adult. As I look back, I had no clue what love was. I did not even love myself enough to acknowledge that before you can love someone you have to love and respect yourself. That would be the first of many unhealthy relationships that I would have in my life.

At 21 I was arrested and charged with masterminding the theft of a million dollars from the bank I worked at. I sat in disbelief in a jail cell losing my mind. I will never forget the harsh smell of anger, pain, and sorrow that filled my cell. I spent the first 24 hours in solitary confinement wearing a paper robe. I truly felt like I was losing my mind. I had no idea how and why I was there. The charges made absolutely no sense to me. How and why was this happening to me? Why would someone accuse me of masterminding a theft? Why would a co-worker that I barely interacted with choose me as his accomplice? Why? Why? Why? I remember throwing up and crying myself to sleep that night. The cell was cold and loneliness was my roommate. Despair and confusion rattled my soul. The next morning my attorney visited me and said that my bail was set at a million dollars. All I heard was "You are not getting out anytime soon."

I would spend the next week in jail living with criminals. It is incredible how slow time goes by in jail. Minutes feel like hours and hours feel like days. My mind would wander off for what seemed like an hour but in reality when I looked at the clock only 10 minutes had gone by. Every time I called my family or friends my heart would break and my eyes would fill with tears, and the last thing you want to do in jail is cry.

I am so grateful to every single person who accepted my calls and would encourage me to stay strong. I would not speak much because every time I tried to say even one word my voice would crack and I felt like passing out. Knowing that I faced a 25-year sentence was surreal. 25 years? What would I do for 25 years in jail? A week later I was able to post bail and go home. I found myself staring at my mug shot from time to time. My cellmate was bipolar and schizophrenic and she kept a plastic bag of razor blades under her mattress. You think you have had crazy roommates? I cannot believe that I went through that. I truly cannot.

I would eventually have all the charges dropped and my record expunged. God only knows how long and painful that process was. I never told that kid to steal money or told him how to do it. I really never got over the whole situation and spent the next 7 years high and depressed.

I tried going to college but that did not work out. All I wanted to do was party and dance until sunrise. Dancing was an outlet and a way for me to forget my pain and past. My drug of choice was marijuana. I was too scared to try anything else. I felt that I would get hooked and end up dead from an overdose if I used cocaine. For me marijuana provided a sense of calmness and peace. It also allowed me to escape to a world that was serene and peaceful.

Shortly after 9/11 I moved to California, once again with one suitcase and a plan to start over again. I was sick of New Jersey and hurt by all the drama. I thought that if I moved everything would be perfect. My life would get better. Now I realize that it was not New Jersey. It was me. It all came down to how I reacted to the things that happened to me.

Smoking marijuana and partying all night long was not contributing anything positive to my life. It actually was creating more drama. Within weeks of arriving in California I was smoking more than ever and hanging out with the wrong crowd. I was too dumb and in denial to see that I was walking into the lion's den.

I soon ran out of money and realized that I had to get a job and get my act together. However, I was involved in an abusive relationship that had gotten so bad that one night I found myself being dragged out of bed and was being beaten by a guy I had dated who was in a cocaine induced rage.

It saddens me to think back on those days because I am a mother now and one day my kids will read this or I will tell them about it and I pray that neither of them will make the same mistakes that I made. Chills are running through my body as I type these words. I cannot believe that I am writing my story for millions of people to read. I hope that somewhere, someone will be inspired to see that we are born with unique gifts and talents. No one can steal or take them away from us.

Regardless of our hardships, mistakes and obstacles we can be and do anything we want. Anything. If you want to be a drug addict, you can do that. If you want to work at a job that you hate, no problem, you can do that also. If you want to be in debt and be broke, no problem you can do it. If you want to be with someone that beats you and disrespects you, no problem, you can do it. I know because I chose to do and be all of those things. I could not control my father wanting to kill me, or that kid sending me to jail. I could control how I dealt with it and how to react to it. I chose to dwell in sorrow and have a pity party, get high and live a miserable life.

The final straw was the night that my ex-boyfriend came into my room and this time he had a knife. Thank God someone heard my screams and called the police. That night I packed my bags and drove away.

The next day my broker at the real estate office I was working at sat me down and gave me an ultimatum. I had 15 minutes to decide what I was going to do with my life. He said that if I went back to that apartment I would have to leave the office or, I could promise him that I would never go back and start from scratch and get laser focused on my life and on my goals.

I had been at that real estate office for a year and he had introduced me to Napoleon Hill, and the legendary Jim Rohn. Until then, I had been crashing on friend's couches for 2 years working odd jobs until one day I was introduced to real estate. I fell in love instantly. At the time I was working as a loan officer for a mortgage company and at night I would work at Express. I did not have a place to live so one of my co-workers who had several real estate properties let me live in the vacant houses that he had on the market. Every night I would blow up an inflatable mattress and study all night for my real estate exam.

One day I overslept and was awakened by a realtor who had clients outside waiting to see the house. I would eat a pretzel and lemonade from Wetzels Pretzels every day when I went to the mall for my night shift. During the day I would eat people's leftovers at my office. This was during the real estate boom so title agents and bank reps would drop off food to our office. I would fill my briefcase with bagels and whatever else they brought and I would eat that during the week. My car was my closet, office, break room, refrigerator and sometimes my bed.

I had my mind set on passing my real estate exam and going big in real estate. Let's get back to my brokers office when he gave me the ultimatum. At this point I was sick and tired of my drama. I was working hard and needed a good kick in the butt with a shot of reality.

I left his office, walked outside, looked up at the sky and decided that I was done being a loser. I was not born to be a loser, a pot head and a drunk. I was born to be a powerful woman. I could take all this drama and use it as fuel to light my fire.

I heard the words of Jim Rohn in my head over and over again. I turned around, walked into his office and said "I am done. I am ready to change." Within minutes a realtor at the office offered to let me watch his dads house for a couple of weeks while his father was away on vacation. All I had to do was feed the dog and bring the mail in every day. BAM! There it was, a new beginning. Just like that.

I am a true believer that when you make a decision to do something, God will find a way to help you achieve it. Someway, somehow, people will come into your life and help you. Trust me, it really works that way. You just need to believe. You need to believe in yourself. I do believe that you have to be hungry, and that you have to really want to fight for your dreams. The word excuse does not exist in my vocabulary. I refuse to make excuses. I am on a mission to empower and inspire millions of people around the world to live their dream lives. To go for it! GO BIG! Regardless of their past, you have to dig deep, roll up your sleeves and get dirty. Nothing amazing comes easy. You have to earn it. You have to be worthy of the million-dollar bank account. Flying around the world and watching the sunset on a private beach from your balcony is possible. You just have to be willing to do the work. Paying off your bills and being financially free is a blessing. You have to earn it. I wanted it so bad and I was ready to make it happen. I began to pound the pavement and work really hard as a realtor.

I put together a vision board. I woke up early and read my affirmations for the day. I attended every personal development seminar that was available. I read every book that I could get my hands on. Most importantly, I began to love myself. I decided that I would not date losers, drug dealers, alcoholics, deadbeat dads or bums. I cannot believe I just wrote that! Really? I had to make that conscience decision. WOW. I was so lost that my taste in men was the loser type. Well, I was a loser so; it actually made sense.

I had very little self-esteem. I could not see why a nice guy, with a full-time job and from a nice family would want to date someone like me. A woman who had such a crazy past. Who would want to bring me home to their parents?

About three months into my new life I met my husband. Little did I know that he would fly out to meet me in New Jersey while I was visiting my family for New Year's, get down on one knee and propose. I barely knew him. We had just been dating for three months. This was crazy. He is the most incredible, intelligent, loving man I have ever known. My eyes are swelling up with tears as I describe him. He truly loves me. He does not judge my past. He does not abuse me. He works his butt off so we can live in one of the most beautiful cities in California, Laguna. I live just minutes from the beach. The weather is always perfect and the sunsets are breathtaking. We have two kids, 5 and 4 years old.

I am so proud of myself that I picked a great father for my children. He loves them. He takes care of them. He was there with me changing diapers and feeding them in the wee hours of the night and he never complained.

My children will never know what it is like to have an alcoholic father. They will never see their mom being beaten and cheated on. They will never know what it is like to not have a father. I do not know what it is like to have a father say, "I love you".

When I walked down the aisle there was no father of the bride. There was no father-daughter dance. My children will never meet their maternal grandfather and that is ok. I am at peace with that. I have so much to be grateful for. Those things do not matter.

If you are reading this and you had an abusive father, please know that you did not do anything wrong. There is nothing wrong with you. You are special. You are beautiful. You are unique. You deserve to be happy. I truly hope that the men I dated are now responsible, loving and caring men. Nobody is perfect and we all make mistakes. Wherever they are in the world I wish them the best.

Being able to forgive my Father and all the people who have caused me pain is so liberating. I am free. I am free to move on with my life and leave it all in the past. I began this story saying that my father tried to kill me and it was a blessing. It is. All the heartaches; obstacles, betrayals and mistakes are blessings. They were opportunities for me to learn incredible life lessons.

Those moments are what inspire me to love with purpose. I am working very hard to create an empire. I am on track to be a seven-figure earner in my company. It is a work in progress. It is not going to happen overnight, but I am in total game mode.

I work on myself every single day. I go out and meet new people every single day. I get to know them and listen to their stories. In return I help them find solutions. I am going to achieve wealth and abundance by listening, empowering and supporting people to achieve their dreams.

One of my greatest joys is to see people achieve their goals and see them succeed! It is so awesome and priceless. It is priceless to see a single mom get herself out of poverty and move into her dream house.

I am telling you that the sky is the limit. It is all in your hands. I cannot believe more in you than you believe in yourself. I have struggled with that a lot. I finally realized that I cannot want someone's success more than they want it. I have to focus, work and surround myself with people who are hungry, dedicated, loyal and committed to their goals.

I envision myself opening orphanages all over the world, donating legal services to those who are in jail and innocent. I am on a mission to help as many children as I can to live in healthy and happy homes.

My mother is not a bad woman. She was a victim and was scared. It took a long time for me to do forgive her. I was very angry for many years. She did the best she could. She taught me to work hard and be disciplined. My mother worked three jobs for 40 years. She divorced my father a few months before I got married. She is single and I pray every night that she finds her prince charming. She deserves to be happy because she has been through so much.

This truly is a surreal moment for me. I am literally typing my story for the world to see. It is so wonderful to be able to let it out all out and not be ashamed.

What are your dreams? What are you waiting for? In case nobody has told you, you only live once and that is it. You get one life to live. Live it the way you want to live it. Stop making excuses about why things are the way they are in your life. It is your life. Get off your butt and go conquer the world. The sky is the limit. Love yourself.

Look in the mirror and tell yourself that you are awesome and that you are worthy. You deserve the best in life. Trust me there is enough money for everyone. Thank you for being a part of my dream. As you read these final words know that there is a 16-year-old girl who is scared for her life and never in a million years can imagine that she will one day be living her dream life.

Thank You. I am so grateful that you took the time to read this. It means the world to me. God bless.

BIO

Sandra C. Pascal was born and raised in Tenafly, NJ in 1977. Her background is of humble beginnings. She is the daughter of Colombian immigrants who arrived in America in the early 70's. She lived in Colombia for 3 years and returned to the US alone when she was 18-yrs-old. At 22, she would face a possible 25-year sentence in a federal penitentiary.

In 2004 she moved to California and started a new life. She now lives in Laguna Niguel California with her husband and two kids. She is a top leader in her company and is now traveling internationally sharing her story and inspiring thousands to live their lives to the fullest.

Email at llovemyoils@yahoo.com

BEFORE THE RISE, COMES THE FALL
By: Hillary Vargas

Who we are and where we are today is a process that did not happen overnight. It is ultimately a lifelong, continuing process or path, full of experiences, decisions, failures, successes, trials and tribulations that has gotten us to where we stand presently. The path that led me to follow my life's purpose of becoming an entrepreneur, youth mentor, life coach, educator and founder of a nonprofit organization called Ms. Hillary's Kids has been long and arduous. My life has been a testament that all that is necessary to follow your dreams lies within yourself. This is at the heart of my work and a foundation of my organization, Ms. Hillary's Kids. I established Ms. Hillary's Kids as part of my passion to support and empower youth with learning disabilities, behavioral challenges or those who come from rough or underprivileged backgrounds to reach their full and highest potential. The majority of the kids I mentor are either immigrants or children of immigrants. This is close to my heart because I came from an immigrant family that emigrated from Colombia for the American dream. If it was not for seeing how hard my parents worked and fought to give my brother and I a better future, I would not be the person I am today. My mother's story and perseverance is part of my story as much as hers. Her example greatly influenced the woman I am today and it is why her story is part of my success.

The American Dream

It was in the year 1984 that my mother, at only 24 years of age, would decide to leave her homeland of Colombia along with my father, in pursuit of the American Dream. Because of the civil war and drug-fueled violence, the situation in Colombia had gotten really bad. They left everything behind and got on a plane to Mexico. From there, they would make their way across the U.S.-Mexican border into the United States. They soon made their way to Stamford, CT where they would stay with a "friend" of my grandmother. Shortly after arriving, they quickly realized it did not matter what education or titles they held in Colombia. Here they were seen as nobodies. Noticing they were immigrants, people would in many instances treat them unfairly.

The person they ended up staying with in Connecticut took advantage of the fact they were immigrants and would lock the kitchen and doors on them. The treatment got so bad that they eventually moved and settled in New Jersey. In New Jersey, they would work in factories during the day, clean schools and offices at night or work as waiters. Two months after having arrived in the U.S., my mother became pregnant with me. Without the support of her family, she would have to fight one the biggest battles of her life.

My mom had a very hard pregnancy with me. At birth, I ended up in the ICU for two weeks. The battles would unfortunately not end there. At 18 months of age, I became very ill and experienced a very high fever, which my mother could not bring down despite all her efforts. She would take me to the hospital and the doctors would simply tell her it was a cold and to take me home and continue to give me over-the-counter medication.

After almost three weeks of being sick, the doctors finally performed additional examinations and tests. Soon after, the doctors informed my mother I had been diagnosed with Juvenile Rheumatoid Arthritis. Rheumatoid Arthritis is an autoimmune disease in which the body's immune system attacks the joints. This creates inflammation that results in severe swelling and pain in and around the joints. This illness would make life very difficult and in many instances take away my ability to do simple things like walk, play or simply be a child. This was incredibly difficult for my mother. When she received the news, she just cried. I believe one of the many challenges going through my mother's mind at that moment was the uncertainty since there was not much research on JRA at the time. I would become a guinea pig for many new medications. My father had to become the sole provider for the family since my mother had to take care of me. This would encompass multiple hospital visits, examinations and would see me go through so much pain, yet she never felt hopeless. She would take 3 buses and walk so much, no matter the weather, just to get me to the hospital for my check-ups. Her love and determination to see me better knew no bounds. What my mother showed me first hand were some of Napoleon Hill's principles through her actions. These include applied faith, going the extra mile and overcoming adversity. What she taught me was to never give up, never lose faith and to believe in what you set out to accomplish. She never gave up or lost faith even when she became a single mother. She inspired me to keep moving forward even in my most challenging times.

The "Signs"

Sometimes in life we might not know where we are going but, if we pay attention, there are always signs all around us. I hit a point in my life when everything was going wrong and it continued for a while. I did not know what path God wanted me to pursue and I started to doubt myself. It was not until I had to leave everything I had built in Rhode Island after college, and move back in with my mother in New Jersey at age 26 due to an accident that I found myself completely lost. However, it was during this time where I became familiar with Napoleon Hill's 17 principles for success. It would be my destiny to encounter a table manned by the Napoleon Hill Foundation at an event, without purposely looking, and meet the grandson of Napoleon Hill. At that moment, I knew a little about Napoleon Hill but I had never read Think and Grow Rich or studied his principles of success. I felt drawn to stop by the table. At this point, I only had $200 in my bank account and after seeing all the amazing books, I felt compelled to get them all. So I decided to take a huge leap of faith and spend the only money I had left in my account on these books. I then grabbed my new books and made the line to meet Dr. James Hill, the grandson of Napoleon Hill. He took the book Think and Grow Rich I had just purchased and asked the one question that would later on lead me to my definite purpose. The question was "What is your purpose?" Without thinking, I said, "to make a difference in our youth and leave a legacy". Dr. Hill then said to me, "Then why are you not doing it?" I had no answer. He then took the book I had just purchased and addressed to "Hillary and the Youth!" He closed the book and said to me "I believe in you, look into the certification from the Napoleon Hill Foundation". Little did I know that would be the biggest sign that became the start of an amazing journey in my life. Upon arriving home from the event, I researched the certification program. However, between not having the financial resources at the time, and recovering from surgery as a result of my accident, I could not attempt the certification right then. I made a plan to get to the point where I could have the financial resources to complete the program. When it was my time, I knew it would get done. It took me two years to get to that point but along the journey I never lost sight of the question Dr. Hill asked me that day. I had also read Think and Grow Rich multiple times. I began to implement his philosophies in my life. I still faced adversities at this point in my life but I understood that this was all part of the process of reaching my definite purpose. As Napoleon Hill famously said, "What the mind can conceive and believe, it can achieve". I thought that my purpose was simply to have a mentoring program. Nevertheless, applying the principles of going the extra mile and applied faith, I created my own nonprofit organization called Ms. Hillary's Kids. This dream initially scared me. At first, a part of me did not think it was possible. Then I thought of the words by Ellen Johnson Sirleaf (the first female elected president of Liberia and the continent of Africa), "If your dreams do not scare you, they are not big enough". The reasons not to pursue were easy. I had no experience or knowledge with a nonprofit organization; I needed financial support and my health (RA). Again I found solace in the inspirational words of other leaders, like Robert F. Kennedy who once said "There are those who look at things the way they are and ask why? I dream of things that never were and ask why not?"; And why not? Why couldn't I create my non-profit? I challenged myself. In June 2015, Ms. Hillary's Kids was officially incorporated as a 501c-3 organization.

Ms.Hillary's Kids

The mentoring program of Ms. Hillary's Kids is designed to help youth establish social, emotional, academic and spiritual balance in their lives. Mentees get to network with some of the most successful individuals in their respective fields, including many who know of and follow the principles taught by Napoleon Hill. They also receive opportunities that enable them to move forward toward their dreams and definite purpose. I believe in empowering each of my "Kids" to reach for the highest star and in teaching them that they, not their circumstances, determine their future, and the effect they will have on the world. In joining my organization, students are committing not only to themselves but to their future selves. They are committing to their peers and to me. They commit to dream big, show up, do the work, and make it happen. The foundation to empowering them lies in teaching them Napoleon Hill's principles of success.

Like I was at one point, many of the mentees who join Ms. Hillary's Kids find themselves lost or without a sense of direction. Many do not know what their definite purpose is yet. Others have grand dreams and a definite purpose but feel achievement is unattainable. Nonetheless, through the organization and application of the 17 principles for success they are taught, many of the mentees are beginning to turn their lives around. They are learning firsthand how a positive mental attitude can help overcome any adversities they come across as they work towards their goals and life's purpose. They are establishing mastermind alliances within the organization and among their peers. Through applied faith, they learn to believe in their dreams and not allow anyone to tell them their dream is too big or too crazy to accomplish. Some have battled depression most of their lives and almost lost by trying to commit suicide, but after joining the mentoring program, they are overcoming their demons and pursuing their dreams of attending medical school, graphic design school or traveling the world. Others were told they would never graduate from high school, are not only graduating from high school at the top of their class but are being accepted into prestigious schools like Harvard University.

During my journey of starting the nonprofit, I still found myself facing adversities and challenges. You see, many people thought I was crazy for dedicating my time, energy and financial resources to supporting urban youth. I was told many times that I was wasting my time and my talents. Many pointed to my rheumatoid arthritis as a reason not to pursue this. What others did not understand was that I knew this was exactly my purpose. Like Napoleon Hill once stated, criticism and discouragement from others comes with the territory when pursuing your purpose and your dreams. Our youth is our future. They are our future leaders, doctors, politicians, engineers, musicians, entrepreneurs and artists. Without our guidance, we could be missing out on their gifts and talents that could benefit society and the world. As an old African proverb states, "It takes a village to raise a child". It is up to all of us to come together and help one another no matter our background, religion, culture, socioeconomic status, etc.

Since youth are our future, it is necessary for us to protect and invest in the most vulnerable to plant the seeds of success so our youth can overcome hardships and not become another statistic.

Making a difference

In the journey of fulfilling my purpose, I have felt alone, at times discouraged and questioning whether I could do this. I will not deny that my illness (Rheumatoid Arthritis) made it a challenge as well. During my most difficult days, I often wondered whether I could accomplish my dream because I had to constantly keep my health in check. How could I serve and help others when there were days I could barely move or even get out of bed. I would come to rely on faith, determination and personal initiative to keep moving forward. As mentioned previously, the feeling of discouragement is natural and very likely experienced by all who have pursued their life's purpose or dreams. Nothing in life that is worthwhile will be easy. And just as it took Napoleon Hill 25 years to write Think and Grow Rich, it does not matter how long the journey might take. In my case, just knowing that because of my work a life might be saved or make a difference in someone's life, it makes it all well worth it in the end. I have mentored over 2000 kids and I realize that, because I followed my dreams, I can serve as an example for them to follow. I can teach and show them that their purpose and goals are possible.

Whether we decide to pursue it or not, each one of us has a divine purpose. It may sometimes not be what we expect or what we might have wanted or planned. It is important to know that everyone's purpose is unique and extraordinary and you have a responsibility to fulfill it. If you have a dream, never lose faith and know that, no matter what, no one can ever take away from you the gifts you were born to give this world. The one thing everyone has control of is their mindset. Your mindset holds the key to establishing a path forward toward your goals. Naysayers and negative mindsets are irrelevant in the end. In the spirited words of William Ernest Henley, no matter the obstacles or the challenges, "you are the master of your fate, you are the captain of your soul". Dare yourself to follow your own path towards your dreams and leave a legacy that will make a difference.

Success

The path to success is not the same for everyone. There is no cookie cutter approach or a precise recipe. There are certainly guidelines and principles that can be applied to aid in achieving success but it is never guaranteed on the first attempt. What is key is to maintain a positive mental attitude {PMA} and an unshakeable faith. It can be argued that failure is inevitable. What really matters is how you react to failure and the next steps you take, no matter how many times failure may occur. It is crucial to learn from mistakes and failures and not let them defeat your spirit. Everything lies within yourself and your mindset. Having a definite purpose will lead to a path forward and invite opportunities that will ultimately help you achieve your goal. The mind, like a muscle, can be fed and trained. Knowledge through reading or research is the food source and applying it is the training until it eventually becomes second nature. Challenge yourself to follow your purpose and ask yourself at the end of each day, "What have I done today to live my definite purpose or accomplish my dream?".

I can relate and understand people who have always been told what they could not become or achieve instead of being told that no dream is too big and that the sky is the only limit. It is also important to always remember that the fall comes before THE RISE! I believe that with the right mentorship and the right tools, there is nothing that YOU cannot accomplish!

BIO

Ms. Hillary Vargas is a life coach, motivational speaker, entrepreneur, youth mentor, educator and Amazon #1 best-selling Amazon author. She is the founder of Ms. Hillary's Kids, a non-profit organization designed to support and empower young adults with learning disabilities, behavior challenges or who come from rough or underprivileged backgrounds, as they reach their full and highest potential. She aids them in seeking out the richest soil they can find and planting the seed of their dreams. As they care for the seed, with Ms. Hillary's guidance, they slowly see it begin to grow. They care for it, and nurture it, until one day it blooms like a rose from a crack in the concrete.

Ms. Hillary has also served as an educator in several urban schools in Rhode Island and New Jersey, teaching and engaging teenage students in a myriad of topics. Her true passions are teaching and mentoring, and investing in our youth, as they are the seeds of our future. She has a BA in Marketing and a minor in Psychology from Johnson & Wales University. As Mahatma Gandhi once eloquently said, "Be the change you wish to see in the world", and Hillary Vargas endeavors to change the world through her students and each person she encounters, one at a time. If you would like to get more information please visit www.mshillaryskids.org or email mshillaryskids@gmail.com

Ms. Hillary's Kids

ACCEPT WHAT IS, LET GO OF WHAT WAS, AND HAVE FAITH IN YOUR JOURNEY
By: Gisella Marie Vasquez

There is a really popular song my dad always sang when I was a kid and I am pretty sure you all know it, so do not be shy, you are more than welcome to sing along. The lyrics go like this...

"Just a small town girl, living in a lonely world, she took the midnight train going anywhere. Just a city boy, born and raised in south Detroit, he took the midnight train going anywhere. Don't stop believing, hold on to that feeling."

As I listened to the song over and over again, I had an epiphany and it gave me the inspiration and strength to share a part of me that I have never had the courage to express. I have come to realize that life is definitely a journey filled with lessons, hardships, adversities, heartaches, celebrations and special moments that will ultimately lead us to our destination, and our purpose in life. The road will not always be smooth; in fact, we will encounter many roadblocks. These moments will test our courage, strengths, weaknesses, and faith. Along the way, we may stumble upon obstacles that will come in between the paths we were destined to take. In order to follow the right path, we must overcome these obstacles. Sometimes these obstacles are really blessings in disguise, only we do not realize that at the time.

Growing up I have always known I wanted to do something great, to be somebody that would make a difference, to be my own boss, invent something or find a cure for cancer. As a kid I was very outgoing, carefree and ambitious. I would talk about all the things I wanted to do and accomplish. Pictures of faraway places around the world would fill my bedroom walls and served as a reminder of how I envisioned my life to be. I would daydream and get excited knowing one day all my dreams would come true.

My mother is a doctor and my dad is a businessman. I watched how hard they worked to give my brother and I a comfortable and good life. I saw how involved they were in the community and the many lives they touched and changed. I remember helping out my mother and grandfather at the skin clinic during the day and tagging along with my dad to business meetings at night. My dad would constantly talk about his vision for the family business he built. I started to see it just like he did and I saw myself making his vision come true knowing that one day I would take over to continue the family legacy.

When I was 14 I found a passion for cooking and decided I wanted to take up culinary arts for college so I could become a chef and open up my own restaurant. Although my dad was very supportive, my mother on the other hand came from a family of Doctors and nurses and urged me to complete my degree in nursing and proceed to medical school if I wished. She would always tell me a nurse can always be a businesswoman but a businesswoman can never be a nurse.

Looking back at my life I thought I had everything planned out. I was going to finish nursing school, move to the USA, work for 10 years, save money, start my own business, retire from nursing by 30, move back to the Philippines & continue the family business so my parents could retire and travel. I was 20 when I left the Philippines and within less than a month I got my first job at a nursing facility. I started to work and save money just as I had planned. I decided to also get a part time job so I could save more. Although I saved money, I started to spend a lot too. I felt like I deserved to live life, explore, enjoy and have fun because I worked so hard. I lost sight of my goals to the point that I was not saving anything. I would spend $5,000 in one night at a club or going out of town just because I knew I could make it up the next two weeks by picking up extra shifts at the hospital on the weekend. After 6 years of being a Registered Nurse, my plan was working. I had saved $80,000, opened up my own restaurant in the Philippines and was definitely having fun. People would tell me; "Do not work too hard, Gisella you are still young, just enjoy your life". I just smiled every time someone would tell me that and, to be honest, I really did not care what they said and did not bother to listen. In the back of my mind I would think to myself - Well this is my life I will live it the way I want to and why slow down now? Life is great! Who says I am not enjoying myself? Everything is the way it is supposed to be and in 4 years I can fulfill my plan and my families plan of running the business back home. I felt like I was on top of the world, successful, making great money, being able to do what I wanted when I wanted. I bought whatever I wanted and provided whatever my family wanted. It was such a great feeling to be able to buy gifts and send money to my family all the time even if I did not have to but because I wanted to. I loved my job, I was finally working at the hospital I had always wanted to work at since the moment I walked into it. I was happy because I was making a difference in other people's lives. I was excited about life and planning my next adventures. I was working hard and playing harder. I felt confident, powerful, accomplished and on track. I felt invincible and unstoppable and that nothing was going to happen to me.

Mark Twain said the two most important days in your life are the day you were born and the day you find out why. February 9, 2014, 12:34 pm was the day that changed my life forever. It was an ordinary Sunday. My friend and I got into my car and less than a mile away from home we got into a terrible car accident. The other vehicle slammed right into my side. We got T-boned at the intersection. My body literally felt like it was lifted up in the air, thrown to the passenger's side and pulled back down by my seat belt yanking me back to my seat. It happened so fast; all I could feel was the adrenaline rushing through my veins and my heart pounding out of my chest. It was not until a few days later that I felt a bump on the back of my head that was sore and I started to get dizzy every time I stood up. I ended up hitting my head on the window from the bounce back motion of the car. The impact was horrific. I ended up with a misaligned spine, posttraumatic cyst on my c5 - c6 that impinges on my nerves causing numbness in my upper extremities and a head concussion that later resulted in mild seizures.

It was a long 6-month battle between me, myself and I. I hated the feeling I got every time I closed my eyes. My mind kept flashing "alternate reality" scenarios in my head. These were horrible mini movies with different endings. As I watched the replay of my accident, a sense of doom overwhelmed me and I could not sleep for days. I would stare at my ceiling, drowning in my thoughts. I asked myself "Why?" and "What if" questions over and over again. Why me? What if I took a different route? If I were seconds behind would things have happened this way? Would my life be different? Hundreds of other questions started to cloud my mind. What are you going to do now? How are you going to survive? How will you pay your bills if you cannot work because of your injuries? How will you provide for your family? How could you be so stupid, careless and irresponsible? I would say to myself; "You are nothing but a disappointment like you've always been. You are never going to be the same. You are worthless and helpless. You are not good at anything. What makes you think you will be successful?

There were days I would literally slap myself to snap out of all the destructive thoughts racing through my mind. I became obsessed with fire. I would light up a candle and stare at it for hours and when I could not feel my arms and hands, I would put hot wax on my hand or on top of the candle just to feel something. For some reason it reminded me that I was still alive and human.

I was on all sorts of medications; narcotics, muscle relaxants, anti-seizure medications (Norco, Soma, Lyrica, Keppra). The pain felt like constant electric shocks from my neck to my fingertips. I experienced sore sharp pain around my chest and other days it felt like insects crawling on my skin. It was driving me insane. I could hardly lift my head or move my neck from side to side, or to get up from bed without aching. Sitting in the car gave me anxiety, so I did not drive. I did not like asking for help from anyone. I felt like everyone was busy with their own lives and I did not want to bother them to take me to my doctor appointments or physical therapy sessions. I let important things slip through the cracks. I was so used to being independent and doing things on my own that I would not let anyone help me. I knew I needed help but I did not like to admit it. I will be honest it was my pride that stopped me. So I just laid there crying and doing nothing. I allowed my thoughts to consume me. I felt empty and there were nights the thought of leaving this world was better than feeling this helpless, hopeless and scared. I started to write down everything I was feeling and going through hoping it would help free myself from all my thoughts.

On April 11, 2014 I wrote:
"I have been talking to myself lately and I am not a nice person. I always seem to put me down. Every time I get the courage to climb out of my hole, and make even the slightest attempt my alter ego is right there looking at me with her arms crossed saying;

'It is always your fault. Why do you think you can get away with everything? Grow up and take responsibility. You are just fooling yourself. You are not worthy of success! You will never be happy again. What makes you think your life will ever be the same? You had it once and now it is gone. Everything is gone! You are nothing! I can go on and on.'

They are right. I am weak. They said that over the phone today. They did not even ask me how I was feeling or even how my day was. And before 1 could say anything they started to point out every single thing I did wrong and that I was not helping myself. The words "Get over it. It has been two months already. You should stop complaining and just move on" hit me hard. It was easy for them to say that, they are not the ones going through this. They are not the ones who are far away and alone. To them, any sign of weakness, even talking about your feelings was unacceptable. I hung up the phone after I screamed at them. I do not remember everything I said but I am pretty sure it was not nice and it probably hurt. I did not care. I was hurting more.
I do not know how or where I should pick up and move on. Everything that I knew I was capable of doing or being was gone. Honestly, I just wanted someone to talk to and understand what I was feeling because even I could not understand myself. I wanted help, a hug, and someone to tell me everything was going to be ok. But I got nothing. Great, there she goes again, make her shut up, make her stop already. I am so confused. Is this the medication or is this me? Please, someone, anyone help me!"

From that moment on I isolated myself from everyone. I did not go out. I did not eat much. I started to become weak and I would skip doctor appointments and physical therapy. I did not pay my bills on time. I just did not care. I trapped myself in the four corners of my room and in my head. I was numb, cold and felt empty. I would drink hard liquor and medications and just sleep. Some nights I wondered if I would wake up the next day. I numbed myself from any emotion so I would not get hurt. Besides, detaching myself from everyone and everything felt so much better than facing reality. I started to disappear physically, mentally, emotionally and spiritually.

One day I looked at myself in the mirror and tears started running down my face. I looked like a dead person walking. I thought; "How could I let this happen?" How could I let it get this far? What was I thinking? I was unsure, confused, anxious, worried, empty and unfulfilled. My heart started to palpitate. Each beat was faster and harder. I could not comprehend how $80,000 was gone within 6 months. I did not even have enough to last me the next few days due to the bad decisions I had been making. I did not want to go back to the hospital. I was ashamed and frightened that I might hurt someone due to my condition. Disgusted with what and who I saw, I dropped down to my knees and began to pray. I asked God for forgiveness, strength and guidance. I reached for my Bible and read Corinthians 12:9-10 "My grace is sufficient for you, for my power is made perfect in weakness. I will boast all the more gladly about my weaknesses, so that Christ's power may rest on me. That is why, for Christ's sake, I delight in weaknesses, in insults, in hardships, in persecutions, in difficulties. For when I am weak, then I am strong" As I kept flipping through the pages, verses stood out. One was Jeremiah 29:11 "For I know the plans I have for you, says the Lord. They are plans for good and not for disaster, to give you a future and a hope." In that moment of silence, I realized that God does not put us in situations we cannot handle nor does he put us in challenging situations on purpose but he puts us in situations to teach us, test us, strengthen us and to lead us to where we are supposed to be.

Sometimes in life you have to be a little lost first to find what you are looking for. Not until you are lost in this world can you begin to find the path that God has planned for you. The only way to find yourself is to lose yourself in something greater than you. Having faith, and realizing that God is bigger, greater, and more powerful than us and that He loves us greatly is the first step to living a purposeful and abundant life. The second step is leaving the life you do not want. Sometimes, it takes a very negative circumstance to show you a clear vision of what you want. I can tell you from my own life experience. I had my own plans. I tried to steer my own course, run my own race, play by my own rules and live a life based on other people's approval. I thought I knew who I was and what I wanted to do. Instead, I was living like who I thought I should be or who I thought others wanted me to be. I soon came to realize God has a plan for all of us and we have a unique purpose here on earth.

The following day I found myself sitting in a room with positive and happy people. It was a familiar place that I had once been to months ago but never had the courage to come back until that day. They talked about 3 important books to read and my mentor told me the book I should read first was Think and Grow Rich by Napoleon Hill. As I opened the first page I read "What the mind of man can conceive and believe, it can achieve." When I picked up on the concept that thoughts are things it gave me an "aha moment" that everything I was thinking was either working for me, or against me. I began to realize we always have a choice. If we choose to be negative, we will find plenty of reasons to stop and frown. If we choose to be positive, we will find plenty of reasons to step forward and smile. I learned to accept that if I wanted my life to change, I had to change. And to change my life I must change and control my thoughts. I started to train my mind to see the good in everything and that there was a lesson to be learned. When I finally understood the biggest limitation I faced was the space between my own two ears, everything changed.

I started to dig deep within my soul and I asked God what was his unique plan for me. A feeling of enlightenment and energy just came over me and when you know something is for you it creates a burning desire you cannot let go of. It is a feeling that will keep you going even when you cannot keep yourself going. A fire began to burn within me. I closed my eyes and began thanking God for giving me a second chance to live, telling him how grateful I was for my life, my family, my friends, my team, my mentors, and the blessings and challenges that had made me stronger. I thought about the dreams I had as a little girl and my passion for helping and serving others. I had wanted to make a difference in the world. I wanted to create change for my family and generations to come. I wanted to inspire others to do great things for their future and their lives by sharing a piece of mine.

I believe things happen for us, not to us. My car accident made me realize that so many people wait for something bad to happen before they make a change for the better, so many people live a life of silent desperation and just want to be heard, so many individuals and families suffer from financial stress due to the lack of preparation and planning and so many people never live their dreams and just settle because of fear. Two years ago I was introduced to a great company and opportunity that will allow me to serve and help others, make a difference, be my own boss, have control of my time, limitless income potential, inspire others to better their lives and lead them to do great things, have peace of mind and become financially free. I found a new passion in the financial industry helping families from all walks of life build a better financial foundation, teaching simple concepts such as saving money early versus later, impact of taxes, living without debt, proper protection and compound interest. Things I wish I learned in school. I never thought financial services was a place for me but I saw the great need of financial education in our world today and how the information would allow people to make better sound decisions in their life. Today at 28, I work with an outstanding team known as Dreamgivers Financial and EMPIRE which stands for Empowering & Motivating People to Invest Right Every day - in God, Family, Community, Yourself, Finances, and Giving back with a positive mind, healthy body and balanced lifestyle. We are dedicated individuals set out on a mission to make an impact in the world through awareness and education, expanding our financial and leadership coaching firm throughout the country and the world.

I am blessed to have this opportunity to share my experience with you and how enduring the pain through life's ups and downs and ending up with a misaligned spine, actually realigned my life. Remember everyone has challenges. Everyone feels lost sometimes. You are not alone. The key is using your experiences to grow. The first step may be hard but believe me, you were meant to do great things. Believe in yourself and keep holding on, and as you take the 2nd, 3rd, 4th, and 5th step, eventually when you look back, you will not even see where you started. When you look into the mirror, you will not even recognize the person looking back at you. Where there once was doubt, you will find certainty. Where there once was a person burdened by his or her trials you will find someone who has the courage to overcome anything that comes their way. Where there was once someone who was a slave to their own limitations, you will find a master of their destiny. Napoleon Hill said, "Desire backed by faith knows no such word as impossible." So don't stop believing. Keep going. Keep running. Don't stop. Have faith in your journey.

BIO

Gisella Marie Vasquez was born on December 11, 1987, in Albany, New York, to business owner Joe Marie Vasquez from Bacolod, Philippines and Dr. Peladiza - Arriola Vasquez from Cebu Philippines. She lived in Florida, USA before moving to Cebu, Philippines at the age of 10.

She continued her education at the Cebu International School and completed high school at the Sacred Heart School for Girls. She was active in school: class president, member of the student council, and was a soccer and volleyball varsity player. She enjoys singing and dancing, cooking, participates in music events and fashion shows to benefit the community and likes to spend time with family and friends at the beach. While growing up, 28-year-old Gisella always wanted to be her own boss and go into the restaurant business for her love of cooking and food but her mother encouraged her to become a nurse. Graduating in 2008, from Cebu Doctors University with a Bachelor's Degree in Nursing. She moved to

Los Angeles, CA at 20 years old and worked as an RN for six years – a supervisor in Glendora charge nurse in Kindred Baldwin Park and ICU nurse at City of Hope. "I loved being a nurse and helping people," she says. Crowned Binibining Kalayaan 2015 for Kalayaan Incorporated a Filipino - American non-profit organization that performs charitable activities to benefit the poor and distressed. She participates in several community projects and actively involved with different philanthropic groups and foundations that help individuals fighting cancer. She played a big part with affiliated foundations in the relief program during Typhoon Yolanda that affected part of her grandparents' hometown.

A major car accident in February 2014 changed the course of her career and perception in life, leading to another path and passion in the financial industry. In less than a year, she quickly rose to the ranks of Senior Marketing Director helping and educating hundreds of families, working professionals and business owners create a strategy and plan to reach their goals.

Today, she owns her own restaurant in Cebu, Philippines, sits on the board of directors of their family business and has strategic partnerships in different industries across the globe. Together with **DREAMGIVERS FINANCIAL** and **EMPIRE INC**- Empowering & Motivating Individuals to Invest Right Everyday, they are currently expanding their financial and leadership firm, which focuses on providing strategies (money management, investments, retirement planning and career development) and resources to achieve financial, career, and life success.

"I love connecting and bringing people together. I enjoy helping others get to where they want to be in life and creating great relationships with people. What I love most about what I do is seeing people dream again, lives changing and playing a part in people's transformation to become better versions of themselves."

Through this career change, and privilege to share her journey with other empowering individuals she hopes to make a difference in people's lives and be an advocate to her generation and to the youth. Gisella can be reached at gisellamvasquez@gmail.com or 626-475-0404

FALL DOWN SEVEN TIMES, STAND UP EIGHT
By: Adrienne Mae Yu

Unfair. For many years that is what I thought of life. Have you ever felt like life or God was picking on you? Why is it that whenever you are gaining momentum a setback is waiting just around the corner? Do you constantly find yourself back to square one? A loved one suddenly passed away. You lost your home in the recession. Negative bank account. Your marriage ended. You had a failed investment. I do not know about you but this past decade alone every adversity in my life seemed to follow each other in rapid succession. I may be the queen of mishaps but I hope that through my story you will understand that defeat is not failure until you have accepted it as such.

As a kid my life was extremely sheltered. I come from your typical strict Asian family. For 9 years I was the only child until my younger brother was born. I went to an all-girls Catholic high school. No boyfriends. No parties. No sleepovers. Those were the rules. There was a nanny who chaperoned me everywhere until I was 16. My parents never even bought me a bicycle when I was a kid because they were scared I would get into an accident.

Coming from a family of doctors and nurses I was expected to walk the same road but even as a kid I had dreams of owning a business. I was in first grade when I started a small business selling Lisa Frank stationery and stickers because nobody else had them in the Philippines. The vision I had for my life was not what everybody had in mind for me. Because of my strict upbringing I had one goal and one desire…to be independent. I wanted to have my own business and not have to work for anyone. I wanted to experience life on my own, make my own mistakes and learn from them. There was such a strong desire to leave behind the shelter I had been put in and forge my own identity. At 14, I decided that I want to live in the United States and I was going to do everything in my power to move after high school.

While most of my friends were scared to leave the comfort of living with their families I was beyond thrilled. Of course there was only one problem. My parents thought it was a crazy idea. The answer was no. But I refused to give up at the first sign of opposition. For three years I begged them to send me to the States or to any other city so I could learn to be independent. To show them how serious I was, I never took an entrance exam to any university that was in my hometown. I studied for the SAT just in case they would change their minds and send me to the States.

Among my favorite things to read back then were Sweet Valley University and Archie comic books. They gave me a glimpse of what living independently in the States was like. I was born in New Jersey but grew up in the Philippines so much of what I knew about living in the States was from books, TV shows and summer visits.

Seeing how much I wanted to move out, my parents agreed to send me to the States. It was a miracle. I was 17 when I left the Philippines. I will never forget that day. I was scared to be alone for the first time in my life but I could not believe that my dreams were finally coming true and that got me more excited than anything.

On the very day that I left home, I met my first adversity. Our flight's stopover was in Hong Kong and there was a huge storm. We were told we would be stranded there for a few days. I had never traveled alone. I had never been to Hong Kong and, although I am half Chinese I did not speak it at all. Suddenly, all these questions started running through my head. Should I still go the States? Was this the right decision? What if this a sign that I should just stay in the Philippines? What am I going to do without my parents? I remember calling my mom with a fear that almost took over me. I wanted to ask my mother for a plane ticket back. Then I started thinking about what my life would be like in the States. I could not even cook a meal let alone survive in a country halfway across the globe from my parents! But then this little voice said, "The storm will pass and you will be just fine."

That was my first lesson and it became my mantra. Every single time I am faced with a challenge, adversity or a roadblock I tell myself that it is only a temporary defeat. Sometimes when we are faced with these heavy burdens we feel like there is no way out. The minute we let go of faith is the minute we succumb to failure. People almost always give up right before they are about to have a breakthrough. When the first sign of misfortune hits us and we project all the worst case scenarios instead of just taking the next step that is when we feel most defeated. The truth is we can only take the next step and not the next ten. Fear has been the biggest culprit in ruining people's dreams. If I had called my mom and asked her to buy me that return ticket a decade ago I would not be half the person that I am today. Everything I ever wanted was on the other side of that crippling fear I felt in Hong Kong…. but nothing came easily.

When I got to the States the concept of work was still foreign to me. I was fresh out of high school. My first job at Best Buy was probably the hardest thing I have done since Chemistry class. I had to sell computers with zero experience while juggling college and yet I still managed to be one of the top sales associates at that location.

Living alone at 17 in a foreign land stretched my mind and my limits. In my first year I struggled with adjusting to the culture. It took me a while to learn even the basic things like ironing my clothes, cooking, and laundry. Sometimes I feel like I was forced into adulthood because I had no other choice. There was nobody else to rely on so I had to learn everything on my own. I even kept telling myself that I could not get sick in America because there was no dad to make me some chicken noodle soup.

After a year of living the "American Dream", my mom encouraged me to come home because she knew I was struggling. I told her I was going to give it another shot. I applied and got accepted to an internship at Disney World in Florida. Looking back that was one of the best experiences of my life and I would have missed that if I accepted defeat. It was difficult but I took the next step that I could.

Disney was the place where I learned valuable business skills. Everything needed to run the happiest place on earth was systematic and detailed. I absorbed all that I could while working there because I knew I could use it some day in my business. But it was not all fun. I was getting paid $6.15 hourly at that time and had to pay rent and survive. I had a business exporting cellphones to the Philippines on the side. I made money but I did not know anything about personal finance.

I had started working but I never learned how to manage money so it mastered me. They do not teach you that in school. This was the time when I was introduced to debt. Something I struggled with years down the road. My parents were still helping me out and sending me an allowance from the Philippines but it was not always enough. I started getting credit cards at 18. As soon as my Disney internship ended my mom asked me if I wanted to come home. You can probably tell at this point that I am not the type to give up. I told her I was not giving up and one day I would have my own business.

My parents started to worry about me so they asked me to move to South Carolina where my aunt lived. They asked me to stay with her so I could be with family. That did not last long because I moved out to live on my own. South Carolina was very different from any place I ever lived in. The great thing about it was I started making good money.

There was a time when I worked as an aquatics coordinator for the military base in Fort Jackson. I also worked as a customer service supervisor at Circuit City. There I applied the skills I learned at Disney World. Life got a little comfortable and it took me two years to realize that was not for me and so I took another risk. I moved to Los Angeles. I drove all the way to the other side of America alone. I did the drive in less than 40 hours with only 6 hours of sleep in between. I do not know how I found the guts or the strength to do it but that is something I will always be proud of. Not everybody can say they drove across America by themselves at 20. It is things like these that exercise your persistence muscle. If you have done something scary in your life once the next thing won't be as difficult.

I wish I could tell you that as soon as I landed in California I lived happily ever after but life has its way of knocking you down when you least expect it. After I started settling in Los Angeles I found a great sales job and thought everything was going smoothly. A few months after my move, I had to go back to South Carolina to take care of my car registration. What I thought was a short break turned out to be the scariest days of my life.

I went to the DMV the second day I got back and out of nowhere a police officer arrested me. He handcuffed me right in front of everyone at the DMV. I am sure he was explaining why he was arresting me but everything was such a blur. My emotions came flooding out and all I did was cry. I could not even ask him what this was all about because I was shaking and scared to death. I was 20 years old and I had never committed a crime except for speeding. I was very sure of that so I thought he must have the wrong person and he was about to realize that any minute and release me but as soon as he put me in the back of the police car it started to get real. Eventually, when I calmed down, I asked him what was going on because I was so confused. I could not believe the words that came out of his mouth. He told me, "You have been arrested for pointing and presenting a firearm. That is a felony." Was this a joke? I do not think I even knew what felony meant.

This officer was really taking me to jail. I was beyond furious. This was the worst day of my life. Jail was definitely scarier and dirtier in real life. They gave us a cold sandwich and Capri Sun juice as we were waiting to get booked. Everyone there looked like they knew exactly why they were there. One lady said she was booked for prostitution, the other one for domestic violence and another was there for theft. They asked me what I did and I said nothing. They laughed but that was the truth.

I was locked in a cell by myself and was hysterical the entire time. What seemed to be years later an officer knocked and asked me if I needed to use the telephone to call someone who could bail me out. The only number I memorized was my uncle's so I gave him a call and told him what happened. He bailed me out the next day.

Apparently what had happened was that an old friend who I had a conflict with made this false accusation. I have never felt so betrayed in my life. She claimed that one night in my anger, I drove to her house pointed a gun at her and threatened to kill her. In South Carolina, that is enough reason for you to be taken in. They issued a warrant for my arrest because the officer tried to find me but I had already moved to California.

My friend and I had a misunderstanding and I thought nothing of it but obviously she took it to a whole different level. I had no idea how to face this. I have never even held a gun in my entire life! How do I defend myself? Where do I begin? And how could this friend do this to me? It was a grueling month. I could not sleep and I barely ate. I lost my job in Los Angeles. I did not know how to prove myself innocent. Then a miracle happened. After rereading the police report a thousand times I realized that the date she put on her testimony was when I was in Orlando. My mom had sent me a Western Union transfer, which I picked up that very same day. What were the odds of that?

I did not have a copy of the receipt because this was awhile back so I contacted Western Union and they agreed to help out. This entire case dragged on for a year so the whole time I was going back and forth between California and South Carolina. This drained me emotionally, financially and mentally. I kept questioning why this had to happen to me when I did not do anything.

A year after that arrest on the final court date I saw my accuser who had no qualms lying under oath and claiming I pointed a gun at her. I presented my Western Union receipt to the judge, my boyfriend testified that he was with me in Orlando and I presented several character statements from my old supervisors from the military. I was found not guilty and the rest was history. After several thousands of dollars spent on the case and a year of torment I could finally move on.

Who would have thought this would happen to me at such a young age? That experience turned me into a person full of resentment and anger. I lived thinking that everybody was out to hurt me. I could not trust anyone. Back in

Los Angeles I carried all that resentment and frustration with life. I was living with so much shame, hurt and forgiveness.

To mask the pain I started going out, partying, drinking, and traveling. I was in and out of a toxic relationship. Eventually, I lost track of my life. Sometimes I thought of starting a new business but I was not going to achieve that with the way I was living my life. I was hopping from one job to another. Financially, I was a mess and made a lot of poor choices. Debt was piling up and I got to a point where I lost my home and I was living with some friends because I could not get my own place. There were days where I literally had a negative bank account. I was ashamed to ask my parents for help. It felt like even they had given up on me. I was guilty for not being the daughter they wanted and deserved. I was guilty for the person I had become.

There was no direction in my life. I could not see what the next step was. One day I got a surprise call from my aunt in Hawaii who offered to teach me how to run a caregiving agency for seniors. She had that business for many years and she wanted to pass along some wisdom. She wanted me to come to Hawaii to study patient care and attend a nursing assistant program so I could better understand the industry. That call came out of nowhere but it was a chance for me to leave the toxic life I had in California and start all over again. Much of my life has been setbacks and starting from scratch and I was hoping that this would be different. I was hoping that I could finally be stable and live the life I had always dreamed of.

A month after I got to Hawaii, I found out I was pregnant. Again, life caught me off guard just when I was trying to change my life. What was I to do with a child that I did not intend to have? With only a few hundred dollars in my account there was no way I was keeping this child. Telling my parents was not an option either. After everything I had put them through, I was not going to tell them they were going to be grandparents.

I had an abortion at 23. That was not an easy decision to make. It felt like I was backed into a corner and I had no choice. Honestly that was worse than sitting in jail. To this day no pain can match that. In my heart I did not want to do it but my head was telling me to be practical. My head was selfish. I could not even take care of myself let alone another human being. That was something I deeply regret and if I could change one thing in my life it would be that. After the abortion I tried to mask the pain again. I felt guilty. I felt lost. I felt ashamed. I felt miserable. It was not until I moved back to California and started going to Saddleback Church that I confronted all these issues.

I believe some bad things have to happen in order for the good things to fall into place. The most beautiful thing that happened to me because of that was I came to know God. I started a relationship with Him. I turned to Him because I had nobody else to turn to. He became my best friend. Slowly I forgave myself and trusted Him. When you release your pains, hurts, and struggles in life to a Higher Power you become strong. This became the turning point in my life. I have more faith today than I have ever had because of all the trials and challenges I faced. I started having faith that God would restore my life. It has been 3 years since I walked with God and my life has dramatically changed.

After Hawaii, I decided to take control of my life. Forgiveness and humility were two things I had to learn to keep going. They are both crucial to overcoming every adversity I had to face. I became humble enough to begin again. As difficult as it was I also learned to forgive myself. It is easier to process your weaknesses to see what steps you can take to change your situation. If we do not take personal responsibility, we can never move forward and take the next step. This is not to say that we should live in guilt. That is one place you do not want to be in. We have to come to a place of acceptance so we can let go. I owned up to all my mistakes in the past and released the shame and guilt that had been holding me back.

I taught myself personal finance, got out of debt, learned how to save and I am more blessed today than I ever have been in the past. Through church, I go to nursing homes and participate in worship services for seniors. At 25, I started a caregiving business in Southern California that helps take care of seniors in their homes. I never gave up. Life tried to knock me down so many times but I kept going because I knew nothing was permanent.

Napoleon Hill said that faith is the only antidote to failure. When you keep that faith alive and you decide to take action no matter how hard more will be given to you. Not just more challenges but also responsibilities. You will be trusted with much if you have been faithful with the little. Just remember that everything changes when you see challenges as blessings.

BIO

Adrienne Yu was a teenager driven to forge her own life and her own story. At 17, she moved to the United States from the Philippines and decided to live on her own. Growing up in a typical strict Asian family, Adrienne developed this deep longing for independence. She thought that life away from her parents meant freedom. But instead of freedom, her life was met with difficulties the day she decided to step out of her comfort zone. Adrienne had to learn how to live on her own and do everything for herself because she had nobody to help her. Can you imagine a teenager alone in a foreign country? It was both overwhelming and stressful. Later on she realized that her life was from freedom and it felt more like she was in chains. The guilt, shame and pain that she carried dragged her into a vicious cycle of partying and drinking. Her life turned into a complete mess almost overnight. She went from medical school dreams to nothing. At first she thought life was unfair and she did not know how to pick up the pieces. She found herself in jail and falsely accused at the age of 20. She lost her job, used credit cards as her source of income and got into debt. Along the way, she made bad decisions and oftentimes found herself alone, depressed and just about ready to give up. But she never did. In one of her life's lowest points, she turned to God and her life changed completely. She learned from her mistakes and did not let them stop her from living the life she knows God has planned for her. Adrienne learned how to use her guilt and her pain to spring her forward and help others learn from her story. Her life was a series of setbacks but through the grace she found her perspective changed and she saw every adversity as a chance to becoming stronger. When you face defeat you either see it as stumbling block or a stepping-stone. She went from broke and broken to restored and she's helping people do the same. Today, she is an entreprencur and an active member of Saddleback Church where she volunteers her time to serve the elderly in her community. Adrienne is a beach lover and a travel bug.

Adrienne can be reached at adriennemaeyu@gmail.com or call at 949-526-4248

NAPOLEON HILL BIO

NAPOLEON HILL

(1883-1970)

"Whatever your mind can conceive and believe it can achieve."
- Napoleon Hill

American born Napoleon Hill is considered to have influenced more people into success than any other person in history. He has been perhaps the most influential man in the area of personal success technique development, primarily through his classic book Think and Grow Rich which has helped million of the people and has been important in the life of many successful people such as W. Clement Stone and Og Mandino.

Napoleon Hill was born into poverty in 1883 in a one-room cabin on the Pound River in Wise County, Virginia. At the age of 10 his mother died, and two years later his father remarried. He became a very rebellious boy, but grew up to be an incredible man. He began his writing career at age 13 as a "mountain reporter" for small town newspapers and went on to become America's most beloved motivational author. Fighting against all class of great disadvantages and pressures, he dedicated more than 25 years of his life to define the reasons by which so many people fail to achieve true financial success and happiness in their life.

During this time he achieved great success as an attorney and journalist. His early career as a reporter helped finance his way through law school. He was given an assignment to write a series of success stories of famous men, and his big break came when he was asked to interview steel-magnate Andrew Carnegie. Mr. Carnegie commissioned Hill to interview over 500 millionaires to find a success formula that could be used by the average person. These included Thomas Edison, Alexander Graham Bell, Henry Ford, Elmer Gates, Charles M. Schwab, Theodore Roosevelt, William Wrigley Jr, John Wanamaker, William Jennings Bryan, George Eastman, Woodrow Wilson, William H. Taft, John D. Rockefeller, F. W. Woolworth, Jennings Randolph, among others.

He became an advisor to Andrew Carnegie, and with Carnegie's help he formulated a philosophy of success, drawing on the thoughts and experience of a multitude of rags-to-riches tycoons. It took Hill over 20 years to produce his book, a classic in the Personal Development field called Think and Grow Rich. This book has sold over 7 million copies and has helped thousands achieve success. The secret to success is very simple but you'll have to read the book to find out what it is!

Napoleon Hill passed away in November 1970 after a long and successful career writing, teaching, and lecturing about the principles of success. His work stands as a monument to individual achievement and is the cornerstone of modern motivation. His book, Think and Grow Rich, is the all-time best seller in the field.

The Seventeen Principles

1. **Definiteness of Purpose**
2. **Mastermind Alliance**
3. **Applied Faith**
4. **Going the Extra Mile**
5. **Pleasing Personality**
6. **Personal Initiative**
7. **Positive Mental Attitude**
8. **Enthusiasm**
9. **Self-Discipline**
10. **Accurate Thinking**
11. **Controlled Attention**
12. **Teamwork**
13. **Learning from Adversity & Defeat**
14. **Creative Vision**
15. **Maintenance of Sound Health**
16. **Budgeting Time and Money**
17. **Cosmic Habitforce**

www.ingramcontent.com/pod-product-compliance
Lightning Source LLC
LaVergne TN
LVHW051524070426
835507LV00023B/3297